D0854711

30130 146320725

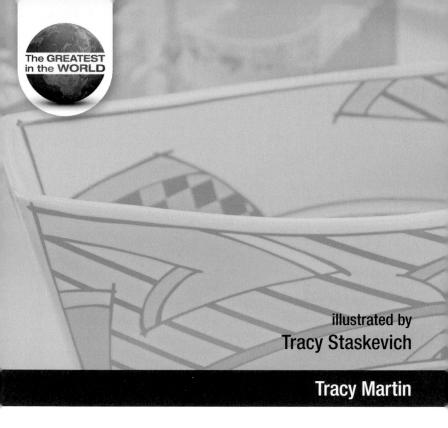

The GREATEST in the WORLD

illustrated by
Tracy Staskevich

Tracy Martin

The Greatest
Collecting
Tips in the World

A 'The Greatest in the World' book

www.thegreatestintheworld.com

Illustrations:
Tracy Staskevich

Typesetting:
BR Typesetting

Cover images:
© Dennis Chinaworks, © Lulu Guinness, © Susan Brewer
© Ektra courtesy of www.fotolia.com

Copy editor:
Karen Darlow

Series creator/editor:
Steve Brookes

Published in 2008 by
The Greatest in the World Ltd, PO Box 3182,
Stratford-upon-Avon, Warwickshire CV37 7XW

A CIP catalogue record for this book is available from the British Library
ISBN 978-1-905151-42-4

Printed and bound in China by 1010 Printing International Ltd.

To my dearest Rod, you were so right,
"Now is called the present because it is a gift"
and to wonderful Brian, who was one of the
greatest influences on my collecting life.

I will never forget you both as you will always
share a place forever in my heart.

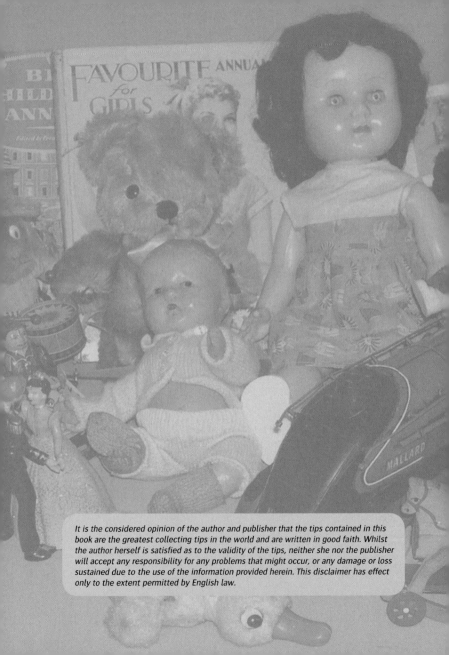

Contents

Foreword by Eric Knowles

When Tracy Martin told me of her intention to write this book and then asked yours truly to write a short foreword, I have to shamefully admit that my decision to agree was, in no small way, influenced by the promise of such a copy as you are now holding in your hand.

Having known Tracy for several years and worked with her on the BBC's *20th Century Roadshow* as well as ITV's *This Morning*, I was quick to realise that, despite her relatively tender years, if anyone had the prerequisite knowledge to write a book of this nature with real authority it was Ms. Martin. No doubt her role with Stacey's auction house continues to be an important factor when it comes to keeping a watchful eye on the market trends.

After more years than I care to remember working in the world of fine art, antiques and collectables I have found myself in regular contact with all manner of fellow valuers and experts. Consequently, I think it's fair to say that I have developed an instinct for recognising 'them as know from them as would have you believe they know' and so can confirm that Tracy Martin is in a league that has to be taken seriously. With her finger well and truly pressed upon the pulse of a rapidly moving market, Tracy has a rare gift for being able to use her vast knowledge whilst maintaining a real passion for her subject.

This is a book to help you get the maximum enjoyment from collecting in a marketplace that offers a bewildering choice and can often seem only too ready to relieve you of your hard-earned cash.

Enter Tracy ... to act as your personal guide, to help you track down bargains at boot sales and offer advice when it comes to bidding at auction. She puts you in the know about all manner of present day potential collectables and introduces an array of items perfect for children to collect.

However, where this book really does score, is in its ability to cover such a wide range of topics and to offer a no nonsense approach when it comes to advising you what Tracy considers to be value for money.

Now, that just might be a Lulu Guinness handbag or possibly a contemporary vase by the much talented Sally Tuffin of Dennis Chinaworks in Somerset, not forgetting the other many talented artists and designers that operate both here in the UK and around the world.

Having seen Tracy's tip-of-an iceberg collection, I can confirm that this lady really does practise what she preaches. Add to that the skill of a seasoned journalist and you end up with the perfect candidate to offer *The Greatest Collecting Tips in the World*. As a result, I am only able to add one single tip of my own, and that is ... if you haven't already bought a copy of this book, then just make sure you do!

Good luck!

ERIC KNOWLES, F.R.S.A.

A few words from Tracy …

A very common disease known as collectavitus has been known to attack when you least expect. Beware – this fascinating new hobby will take over your home, your life and your finances. On the positive side, however, it will also bring a host of new friends, exciting experiences and adrenaline rushes which are better than any rollercoaster ride.

An avid collector for 35 years – I had no choice, I was born into a life of clutter. My parents have always been monstrous hoarders, filling their lives with various knick-knacks, and every birthday and Christmas I would receive another little ceramic bunny to add to my ever-growing collection. At an early age I realised that no amount of 'cold turkey' would ever stop me collecting or beat the thrill that I experienced when hunting out treasures, as the collecting disease was inherent and ran in the blood.

Little did I imagine, during those childhood days, that I would eventually be one of those fortunate people who is able to turn their hobby into a career. After winning a well-known television programme, Boot Sale Challenge, I landed myself a regular column with Collect it! magazine, before becoming a colleague and friend to Lorne Spicer with whom I worked for five years. Now I write for a host of magazines, travel the world giving lectures on my favourite subject and work as a collectables' valuer at my local auctioneers, Stacey's.

One of the highlights of my career to date was being asked to write this book, *The Greatest Collecting Tips in the World*. It fulfils a lifelong dream of passing on my knowledge, skill and passion to other like-minded people. Full of useful tips including tricks of the trade, where to buy and digging out hidden treasure, this book will, I hope, not only teach you the ropes, but also show you how to put your new-found knowledge into practice.

So sit back and get ready as that collecting bug is about to bite.

Happy collecting!

Tracy

> **Collecting is my joy; it gives me great satisfaction.**

Ursula Andress

Life as
a collector

chapter 1
Life as a collector

Collecting is a serious business which should not be entered into lightly, so when you are first contemplating life as a collector there are a few things you need to take into consideration. It's a life-changing hobby, with drawbacks as well as rewards, and all sorts of complications in between. So here are some tips which will, hopefully, make your collecting experiences enjoyable and fun rather than the alternative which could turn out to be miserable, unmarried and skint!

Reasons for

Collecting is just the best! Not only are you entering a world where you'll meet a whole new set of interesting people, but you'll also pick up all sorts of fascinating information as part of your research. Then there is the excitement of hunting out your items at auctions, boot sales, fairs and collectors' centres – something you have possibly never even considered doing before.

Of course, there is the serious side of making sure you know exactly what you are buying but what better excuse is there for allowing yourself to spend copious amounts of money on collectable goodies to fill up all those empty cabinets, shelves and rooms around your home.

Reasons against

However, there are also downsides to consider. Before starting it is important that you make sure you are prepared for that adrenaline rush that surges through the body when you spot a must-have bargain or even something that costs the earth. This overpowering feeling is common amongst collectors, and has led to additional complications. People have had to build extensions, or even move house in order to accommodate their addiction for buying anything and everything that is deemed collectable.

So my advice is, think carefully. Can you afford it, is there enough room and do you really need it? It's not worth the upheaval of moving house or ending up bankrupt.

Partner's permission

I know it sounds crazy, but you really do need to ask the person or people that you live with if they are happy for you to start collecting. Not only will you be filling their home with your new treasures, spending every penny that you earn and locking yourself away to trawl internet sites, but their weekends will be taken up with early morning boot sale hunting, intense auction bidding and as many collectors' fairs as possible. Their life is no longer their own – it's part of yours. So please, please, please make sure that everyone who might be affected by your new hobby is willing to participate, otherwise you may find yourself responsible for a family mutiny.

Display or hide away

People never realise until too late just how addictive collecting can be, so make sure you can house the items you buy by displaying them properly. There is no point in buying your little treasures then keeping them tucked away in boxes under your bed, in the wardrobe or, even worse, in the great black hole we call the attic. Invest in a nice display cabinet or choose one room to fill up with your new found collectables. You are collecting because these items give you pleasure and you enjoy looking at them, not as possible investments for the future.

Where to begin?

Once you have taken the above tips into consideration and everyone is prepared for this all-consuming new pastime, the next step is knowing where to begin. Most people, even the most tidy-minded amongst us, find they accumulate a collection of something over the years. It may have happened by default, through an inheritance or simply because you've stored the children's toys away in the attic but before venturing out into the big wide world, take a look round the home and see what you have.

Uncover every stone

When searching the home make sure you don't leave a stone unturned. That simply means check out every nook and cranny. You never know what you might find hiding at the back of a cupboard, and then of course there is the attic, garage, and shed. Ensure that you also keep an open mind; something you discover may look completely worthless to your untrained eye but believe me this is usually how the gems are uncovered.

Treasure or trash

The home can hide a whole host of objects which in the past have been ignored. It is surprising what your childhood Barbie doll could be worth or that Cornish **Troika** vase which you bought on holiday back in the 1960s. Nearly every room has the potential for some collectable goodies. Look at things in a new light, not as pain-to-clean dust gatherers but as little treasures that suddenly have collectable appeal.

- Living Room
  Look at the books, records and ornaments to see if any have collectable appeal.

- Kitchen
  One of the hottest subjects is kitchenalia, so see if you have anything that slots into this category.

- Dining room
  Check out the drinks cabinet for Breweriana (drinks advertising mementos), 1950s kitsch dinner services or even those old wine glasses that you never use.

- Bathroom
  Not too much usually found here but you never know, there may be an original bottle of Beatles talc!

- Master bedroom
  Perfect for vintage clothing, handbags, perfume bottles, compacts, jewellery and cosmetics.

- Children's bedroom
  Toys, teddy bears, dolls and ornaments.

- Garage
  Old bottles, car mascots and badges.

- Shed
  Anything hidden away such as old tools and garden ornaments.

- Attic
  This could turn out to be the best of the lot, a real treasure trove.

- Miscellaneous
  Anything from old dial telephones to that strange shock machine that great aunt Lily passed down. You will be surprised at what you can find.

My childhood collection of Royal Doulton Bunnykins figures became not just sweet little ornaments that filled shelves, but a desirable and valuable collection which I began to expand on.

FACT

The Troika factory was established by Benny Sirota, Leslie Illsley and Jan Thompson in February 1963. All three raised £1,000 each to take over the Wells Pottery at Wheal Dream in St. Ives. Together they produced a range of decorative and sculptured art pottery that was aesthetically pleasing rather than being particularly functional. Many of you will recognise these pieces by the innovative textured decoration and of course the Troika signature, which can be found on the base of all their wares. Items produced by Troika include wall plaques, vases, jam pots, tribal masks and ashtrays. The factory ran for 20 years before finally closing it's doors in 1983.

What's hot and what's not?

If you are not lucky enough to own anything very collectable, then think carefully about what you would like to collect. Visit collectables fairs, auctions and internet sites to get some inspiration. It's like buying a house, the minute you see what you want nothing else will do and this is when the addiction starts to take hold.

Collecting trends are as fickle as fashion so look to things that are sought after now or could well be in the future. Top quality craftsmanship will always stand the test of time as will childhood nostalgia and classic design.

Because you love it!

The golden rule of collecting is 'buy it because you love it' – don't ever purchase something in the hope that it may increase in value at some point because this isn't guaranteed. You have to live with these items, so make sure you are buying them because they give you enjoyment and pleasure. Who knows, maybe you will hit the jackpot in years to come when your collection has increased in value.

I have trained my collecting tastes over the years and now boast a respectable collection of the British pottery offerings from Dennis Chinaworks in Somerset. Every piece is handmade and painted by a skilled team with their designer Sally Tuffin at the helm. These pieces in my collection are not just beautiful works of art but fill me with joy every time I admire them in the display cabinet.

Start off small

If you're a collectables virgin, you need to start off small. Yes, we would all like to own the rarest item on the market but it's a good idea to start off with easier-to-find, affordable items.

Cheap or chic

Financing a collection is an extremely important factor to consider. These things don't come cheap and the more you crave, the more you buy and then the more money you spend. Set yourself a budget and never pay over the odds in the beginning. Remember, if you are still getting to grips with this collecting lark it's best not to part with huge amounts of money to start with.

Good examples of Clarice Cliff Pottery are almost impossible to find unless you are willing to remortgage the house and buy from auctions and specialist dealers. Start by collecting something more affordable. Who knows, further down the line you might be able to buy bigger and better pieces.

Condition counts

Don't be tempted to buy damaged goods when you first start collecting, no matter how cheap they are – condition really does count. You'll realise, as you learn more, that not all pieces carrying a chip or crack are worthless but generally things that have been broken are a no-no. Make sure everything you buy is in excellent or near mint condition with no sign of chips, cracks or restoration. Also with dolls, teddy bears and vintage clothing make sure they are in really good condition because this can seriously affect the price.

Missing or complete

This applies to many things but especially to toys and games. The value of a piece depends on whether it has all its components. A mint carded 1970s Star Wars figure that has never been played with can command hundreds, whilst one loose without its accessories will be worth a fraction of the price. You only get what you pay for – so before buying check that the item has all its bits.

Boxed or unboxed

Boxed, no question about it. Never, ever cast away anything that could add value or lasting appeal to a collectable. You hear stories of items selling for triple their usual value, just because they were encased in their original packaging and I've seen it happen time and time again. A 1970s Pippa doll, for example, is quite sought after, especially if dressed in an original outfit and will fetch between £25 and £35. But if you still own the box that she came in, then you could expect to realise around £100 for her. Quite a difference in price, I'm sure you'll agree. The same goes for most collectable items – so it is imperative that, where possible, you store away the original packaging as it might come in handy much later.

Priced for packaging

Packaging alone can command a premium especially if it's evocative of a period. So never dismiss the old soap powder box that you found at the back of the kitchen cupboard, or the 1970s bingo game that has been under the bed for years. There are many collectors of packaging who will be dying to get their hands on these priceless items.

Vintage packaging

Some ideas of vintage packaging to look out for:

- Confectionary wrappers (preferably still with the chocolate or sweets).
- Cigarette packets such as Players, Lucky Strike, etc.
- Cereal boxes.
- Cleaning products.
- Food packaging like 1940s powdered eggs or 1960s soup tins.
- Cosmetics containers.
- Board games and jigsaw puzzles (complete if possible).
- Old clothes patterns and sewing needles.
- Matchboxes.
- Medicine bottles.
- Face cream and beauty canisters.
- Talcum powder.
- Perfume and aftershave boxes and bottles.
- Original boxes for toys.
- Christmas decoration boxes.
- Drinks packaging such as Coca Cola, Corona etc.
- Biscuit tins.
- Bubble and chewing gum wrappers.
- Music memorabilia.
- Fashion orientated items, paper bags with shop name etc.

Genuine or fake

Make sure you know your collecting area and can spot a fake. This is probably the steepest learning curve for novice collectors but definitely one of the most effective. I made many mistakes when first starting out and it really does teach you to pay attention next time round... You think you have discovered the find of a lifetime, an original set of Carltonware Guinness Flying Toucan wall plaques. Excited, you take them home and then start to really examine them. The paintwork looks too good, with clean, defined lines, the colours are far more vivid than expected – hang on, the maker's mark on the back doesn't match the age it is supposed to be. Yes, you have paid out an extortionate amount of money for a fake! You won't be doing that again; live and learn – mistakes happen to the best of us and it gets easier as you become more experienced and knowledgeable about the things you're collecting.

In the early days, I bought a beautiful tube-line Charlotte Rhead jug from an internet auction site. Not having enough knowledge, when the piece arrived I thought it was okay, but a couple of years later when I tried to resell it I found out that it was a fake reproduction copy and so lost a lot of money.

Knowing your limit

As you're probably already discovering, collecting is an addiction so make sure you know your limit. Restrict yourself to buying a couple of pieces a month rather than jumping in at the deep end and buying everything and anything associated with your collecting area. That way you won't get carried away and make too many mistakes.

Let the battle begin!!!

So now you know all about the personal drawbacks and advantages to collecting. You have ransacked the house, checked your bank account, and asked him or her indoors if it is okay to fill your home with clutter. The green light is on and it's time to do battle. But be careful, this is a tough industry and everyone wants a piece of it. Those crazed collectors are desperate to secure the same pieces as you are for their prized collection.

Summary checklist

- Make sure everyone knows about your new hobby.
- Ask your loved ones' permission.
- Make room to display your new treasures.
- Check your home, garage and shed for anything that might trigger off an appealing collection.
- Research your chosen area properly.
- Set yourself a realistic budget when starting.
- Always check condition, that the right pieces come with the item and whether it is boxed or unboxed.
- Learn how to spot a fake.
- Restrict yourself to buying just a couple of pieces per month to start with.
- Be prepared for that 'collectavitus' disease that is known to strike, as the adrenalin rush and 'must-have' feeling takes hold very quickly.

"Collecting has been my great extravagance. It's a way of being. I collect for the same reason that I eat too much – I'm one of nature's shoppers.

Howard Hodgkin

Knowledge
is power

chapter 2
Knowledge is power

Before you even consider rushing out to buy your collectables you need to gain some basic knowledge first. If you put in the groundwork, not only will you make much more of a success of your collecting, but you will get much more enjoyment out of it, too. Collecting is a complicated and vast subject, including everything from coins and stamps, ceramics and glass to clothing and toys, so it is important that you learn about your preferred areas of interest before you start splashing your cash.

Up-close and personal

The best way of learning is to actually see things in the flesh. Get out there and visit as many collectables centres, auctions and fairs as possible. Handle the items even if you don't intend to buy, as this gives you an indication of how a piece should feel. Nothing beats actually examining an item up close. Believe me, once you have laid your hands on a piece it really will stick in your mind.

Whilst working on the BBC's *20th Century Roadshow* and, more recently, in my career as an auction valuer I have learnt far more by being able to handle these wonderful items. Last year I discovered three rare Italian porcelain Lenci figurines at a lady's home. I had to conceal my excitement at seeing such wonderful works close up. These pieces will forever be in my memory.

Reference books

Buy as many reference books as possible. Written by experts in their field, these are the bibles as far as collecting goes. There are all sorts to choose from so if you're interested in a very specific area, look for specialist books on the subject. If however, you are still undecided on your collecting area then it's worth buying some of the more general books, such as the Miller's guides, to give you a steer. These handy books will not only give you an idea about what to look out for but usually have in-depth information and price guides. Bear in mind, though that these price estimates are not set in stone. Items are only worth what people are prepared to pay so use the prices in the books as guides only.

Television programmes

There is a wealth of television programmes dedicated to this subject and it is a good idea (and good entertainment, too) to watch and learn through these. Generally, television experts are well-known auctioneers or dealers, who have been in the business for many years. Remember, though, it is not possible to know everything about everything. These programmes can give a useful indication of what is out there on the market and a basic guide on price, but if you're still unsure look to another source for more detailed information.

Subscribe to knowledge

Take a look at the various specialist magazines dedicated to collecting – you'll find them in the larger chains of newsagents. This is the perfect way to gain knowledge and stay abreast of the ever-changing market trends. If you have difficulty tracking down the magazine that you are after, it's worth taking out a subscription. That way you will always know what's hot and what's not in the collectables world.

Lectures and workshops

An effective way of gathering information is to check your local paper regularly to see if any collectable or antiques experts are holding lectures in your area. You will be surprised how many of them actually travel the country giving talks on their areas of expertise. Not only will you learn a lot from the designated expert, but you'll also get the chance to ask them questions.

I always try to attend any lectures that take place in my local area, especially if the speaker is a well-known television expert. And when you are on holiday, find out if there are any special events or lectures taking place, especially if you're going on a cruise. I, along with many other experts, regularly give collectables talks onboard cruise ships. When you're relaxing on holiday it's a great time to learn something new.

Working holiday

You don't have to leave dry land to immerse yourself in the world of collectables and antiques, many travel companies offer weekend and holiday antiques breaks, too. Some include the services of recognised experts who act as your guides and give you their undivided attention whilst you are travelling with them. So, if you are looking for a break with a difference, why not indulge your passion and book yourself on to one of these special tailored holidays?

Expert opinion

Visit your local auctioneers. They know the current market inside out as they sell items on a regular basis. Auction sales are also fantastic places to visit and handle items, especially general sales with a whole host of different items on offer. Try to attend the viewings (usually a couple of days before the actual sale) as this gives you the opportunity to handle hundreds of items without actually having to buy anything. I guarantee you will learn loads – I do every month!

Internet

This is another great source of information and is where I tend to look when I want some hard, instant facts. You can discover a wealth of fascinating information that you may not find elsewhere without even having to leave the comfort of your own armchair. Start off by searching the dedicated collecting sites, or if there is something that you are particularly interested in then use **www.google.co.uk** to see if there are any sites that are dedicated to the subject.

My favourite site (and one that I actually contribute to) is **www.worldcollectorsnet.com** as it covers every collectable category possible, with full articles, discussion forums and updated information on market trends. Not all sites are as accurate and informative as this, however, so remember when looking at information on websites to cross reference any facts as some information can be contradictory.

Internet auction sites

These sites are perfect for checking out current market values. They are becoming increasingly popular and give bang up-to-date prices. Take time to feel your way around the sites, exploring the various categories and checking out what sells well and what is best to avoid. Nowadays, auction sites set the market trends and values, especially for more easily accessible items such as modern collectables, glass, toys and ceramics – use them to your advantage.

Buyer beware! You really don't want to get your fingers burnt on these internet auction sites. Start by using them to research prices before you become part of the auction-buying circle. If you start too early you could end up getting a raw deal.

Learn by your mistakes

I made many mistakes when I first started collecting and it certainly taught me to pay attention next time round. Just be careful, but if you do end up buying a fake piece of pottery, a cloned doll or even something that turns out to be damaged, then take it on the chin and put it down to experience. Even the best of us have been stitched up at some point.

Friendly forums

Remember, you are never alone when you're a collector. There are millions of people out there all doing the same thing. Register yourself with some of the internet discussion forums and chat with other like-minded people. We are a friendly bunch and are more than happy to help you on your way to trouble-free successful collecting.

Collecting clubs

If you are a complete technophobe and haven't the foggiest about how to switch on a computer, let alone check out an auction site or register with a forum, you might feel happier joining a collectors' club. For a small fee, the clubs usually offer a newsletter with all the tips, market trends and information on your chosen collecting area. Some hold open days where you can go along and meet other collectors. These days out are perfect for learning as you can gain a great deal of knowledge from people who are dedicated and passionate about their collecting subjects.

Armed and ready

You won't become an expert overnight, it takes years of learning and experience, but I hope I've at least helped you to get a bit of a head start before you join the world of collectors.

So you are armed with information and are now in a position to go out there and start buying but where do you start? The decision is entirely up to you, but I personally believe that you need to learn to walk before you can run. There is still a lot to learn and, I guarantee, a few mistakes to make along the way.

Mail out

Join as many factory and manufacturing mailing lists as possible. This will give you an insight into what is new on the market, ensuring that you are always abreast of collecting trends, thus keeping your brain in tune to the ever changing market.

Summary checklist

- Handle the items you're interested in at collectors' fairs and auctions.

- Read anything and everything associated with your collecting area.

- Watch and learn with relevant television programmes.

- Attend local lectures and talks by leading experts.

- Check out your local auction house for what is hot and what is not.

- Surf the internet for instant facts.

- Check market prices by looking at the popular internet auction sites.

- Don't be dismayed if you make a mistake, it happens to us all.

- Register with discussion forums to chat to other like-minded collectors.

- Join a collector's club and attend their open days, you can learn heaps by just talking to others and have a thoroughly enjoyable day out as well.

- Join mailing lists to keep abreast of the market.

"Nobody can give you advice after you've been collecting for a while. If you don't enjoy making your own decisions, you're never going to be much of a collector anyway."

Charles Saatchi

Thoroughly modern Millie

chapter 3
Thoroughly modern Millie

Antiques used to be the favoured items but in recent years collectables have taken over. Factories are cashing in and even cosmetics and fashion houses have cottoned on to the power of a limited edition. With so much on offer, how do you know where to start and whether what you buy will be collectable and have longevity?

Supply and demand

Collecting is literally supply and demand. If there is not enough of something to go round then its collectability is increased. So look for items related to your collection that are likely to be in great demand from other collectors.

Limited editions

When collectamania first started you really could get your hands on a small limited edition piece... but it came at a price. Obsessed collectors would queue for hours hoping to secure just one of the pieces on offer. Sadly things have changed now and many manufacturers release limited edition runs of as much as 5,000, thus killing the excitement of winning that limited trophy. Check out the production run before you buy, if it really is as low as 500 worldwide then it is worth running the race.

Remember always to keep the boxes that your items come in, along with any limited edition certificates or paperwork, as this adds to the provenance of a piece.

Time limited

Don't be put off if things are 'time limited'. These items are often made to order and sometimes there are fewer pieces in existence than any limited edition, thus adding to the rarity factor.

General release

General release pieces have a constant run until the manufacturer decides to withdraw the design. Don't let that put you off because they can still become rare pieces in their own right. When Royal Doulton held the licence to produce Raymond Briggs' The Snowman figures back in the 1980s these delightful character collectables were not particularly good sellers. Today The Snowman is one of the biggest collecting areas and the original Royal Doulton examples come at a premium as collectors fight to get their hands on them.

Made in Britain

High production costs in the UK have forced many factories to move their manufacturing to the Far East. As a result collectors across the globe, including USA, Australia and Canada, desperately seek out those rare pieces that are still made by British factories, ensuring that the collector's market is still extremely strong for good quality British pieces. So where possible consider buying British.

When I give lectures many of the audience are international collectors who are eager to purchase those high quality items that are still masterfully produced in Britain.

Pottery and porcelain

One of the most collected areas is that of ceramics (pottery and porcelain). There is no shortage of ceramic delights to collect and although some reputable factories have now ceased production, others are still successfully manufacturing today. Choose wisely, buying only what you like because there are hundreds of factories to collect from and otherwise you will end up like me, with examples from nearly all of them.

Dennis Chinaworks in Somerset puts the great into British. Not only do all their pottery creations tick all the right boxes for collectors but they are the only contemporary factory prestigious enough to have an annual sale of their goods at London's Bonhams saleroom.

Echo of Deco is another family-run ceramics factory based in Lancashire. Father and son team, Malcolm and Russell Akerman, have a passion for Art Deco design which they carefully reproduce from their studio. Examples of their work can be found in collections right across the globe

My own personal favourites:

- Dennis Chinaworks
- Echo of Deco
- Roger Cockram
- Wedgwood / Coalport
- Royal Doulton
- Italian Lenci
- Goldschieder
- Poole Pottery
- Midwinter
- Royal Worcester

Glassworks

If ceramics isn't your thing then how about some of the many glassworks around the globe? I prefer factories which produced in small limited edition sizes because if each piece is handmade or blown it adds to the desirability of the glass. There are hundreds of glass factories and many boast a massive database of loyal collectors. Some of the best producers are based in Britain and many countries across Europe, so take time to choose the factory that fits your own personal taste and don't overlook other factories that may have gone out of business but still have huge standing in the world of collectables.

My own personal favourites:

- Glasform (John Ditchfield).
- Isle of Wight.
- Okra Glass.
- Whitefriars (Geoffrey Baxter Textured Range).
- Italian Murano.

Bronze age

Bronze sculptures have suddenly become all the rage and many skilled artists are trying their hands at casting. Adam Binder Editions is one of the most successful producers of these stunning works of art along with Dinsdale Petch of the Running Dog Foundry in Devon. They don't come cheap, but if you're after quality workmanship at its best, then investing in one or two bronzes may well be a wise move. If the likes of Lorenzl, Ferdinand Preiss and Chiparus from the beginning of the twentieth century are anything to go by, then our modern manufacturers may well be just as sought-after in years to come.

Magical nostalgia

People love to reminisce about their childhood and vintage toys always have collectable appeal. Original pieces are expensive and hard to find, so look at the modern equivalents that are produced today. Giftware Company Roger Harrop produces many children's comic and television characters in resin. Dennis the Menace, Thunderbirds, The Clangers and Camberwick Green are among their more popular ranges. So if a trip down memory lane is what increases your passion for collecting, try to source modern designs based on vintage toys. If ever you come across any of the original vintage toys then you must definitely snap them up.

Look at traditional toy manufacturers which are still producing today such as Corgi, Hornby, Scalextric and Lego.

Boy's toys

Top collectable 'boy's toys' manufacturers, past and present:

- Airfix
- Aster (trains models)
- Bing
- Britains
- Budgie
- Corgi
- Dinky
- Hornby
- Hot Wheels
- Lego
- Lone Star
- Marklin
- Matchbox or Lesney
- Meccano
- Palitoy
- Scalextric
- Schuco (model cars)
- Subbuteo
- Timpo
- Triang

Resin delights

Resin sculptures have become big business in the collectables industry and some of the better-known artists have worldwide followings. The designs of Adam Binder Editions, Robert Harrop and Border Fine Arts are amongst the most collectable – especially the pieces by a good designer or which have been withdrawn. Each one is very different from the next, so look at the designs to see if any appeal to your taste.

Bearmania

Teddy Bears are amongst my favourite collectables. Not only are they absolutely gorgeous but they are loved by all and have a fantastic following. One of the most popular manufacturers is Merrythought, a UK company whose most saleable bear design, *Cheeky* has a massive following in Japan. The German factory Steiff has always been the leader in bear design, but there are also many other manufacturers such as Deans and Boyds, along with hundreds of artist bears which are made by individuals.

> **FACT**
> Margaret Steiff's nephew Richard Steiff was the original creator of the first teddy bear in 1902.

Quick tip

Get clued up on bears with one of the specialist teddy bear magazines. *Teddy Bear Scene*, published by Warners, is one of the best. This glossy monthly is packed full of information and edited by Kathy Martin, one of the country's leading bear experts.

Dolly daydream

Just like their cuddly counterparts, another collecting area with worldwide interest is that of dolls. Many prefer the antique variety but I personally opt for the more modern fashion dolls like Sindy, Barbie and Pippa. This is purely because they bring back memories of my own childhood. When buying dolls make sure that that they are in tip top condition, check to make sure that the fingers haven't been chewed, that the hair plugs aren't missing or the doll hasn't turned a green tinge in colour. These are all worth avoiding.

FACT

The 1965 version of the Midnight Blue Barbie doll (actually dressed in red) sold for a staggering £9,000 at Christie's auctioneers creating a world record for these dolls. The rare pink version wasn't so far behind, it sold for £5,040.

Quick tip

To find out more about collecting dolls, take a look at Doll magazine, a great publication edited by leading expert, Susan Brewer and published by Ashdown.

Raise your glasses

No, it's not just about drinking the booze — but the extensive range of collectable merchandise associated with the products. Advertising memorabilia is hugely popular especially when it comes to drink and the Guinness brand is probably one of the best known in the Breweriana category.

Movie madness

The same goes for big blockbuster films. There was tons of merchandise for the Harry Potter films and The Lord of the Rings trilogy. The top end pieces produced by companies such as Royal Doulton, Royal Selangor and Arthur Price all became must-have items, especially as many of them were associated with each individual film so were only available to buy for a short duration. Remember how prices for the original Star Wars memorabilia hit an all time high – well the same is probable for today's big screen movies.

Stamp collections

I recently discovered the charm of Buckingham Covers. Considered the new marvel of the collectables world, this company produces the most fantastic first-day cover stamps which actually increase in value, especially as most of them carry genuine signatures of well-known and famous people, thus crossing over to autograph collecting. They make the ideal collectable for everyone, no matter what you collect – you will certainly find at least one that fits into your collection. (Also see *Sticking with stamps* on page 125).

> **FACT**
> Tony Buckingham is one of the world's leading authorities on first-day covers and ran the very successful stamp cover company, Benham, until 1997 when he started Buckingham Covers.

Sporting greats

Sports memorabilia, like advertising merchandise, is eminently collectable and very popular. Major sports such as football, rugby, cricket and golf offer endless collecting opportunities. Look out for items associated with a certain date in sporting history or a famous participant.

Autograph hunting

Collecting autographs is another area to consider and can be greatly rewarding. The best way to start is by writing to your favourite television stars and asking if they would be kind enough to send you their signature. Always include a return stamped addressed envelope so they can send the autograph back to you. Of course there is the possibility when purchasing autographs that the signature might not be genuine, however the more time you invest in this hobby the more you will learn how to spot a fake. The best way to get genuine autographs is to go to star studded events and actually ask the celebrity in person. On one of my recent trips aboard a cruise ship, I was delighted to meet the 1966 World Cup scorer Geoff Hurst. He was only too happy to sign a photograph for me, and I had my picture taken with him so it backed up the fact that yes, the signature was genuine and I had met this iconic footballer.

If you are unable to get to celebrity events then there are also reputable dealers and auction houses where you can purchase signed photos. Do make sure that they have the paperwork to back up the signature by asking if there is any provenance and as always if you are a little unsure – do not buy! Wait until you find the autograph somewhere else.

Collecting suggestions

Here are some suggestions to give you a helping hand on what to collect, although there are many more categories to consider.

- Ceramics (pottery and porcelain)
- Glass
- Vintage toys
- Vintage fashion
- Vanity items (powder compacts and perfume bottles)
- Commemorative ware (royal and sporting memorabilia)
- Militaria
- Kitchenalia
- Bottles and pot lids
- Advertising memorabilia (consumer products)
- Stamps and coins
- Bronze sculptures
- Resin figurines
- Autographs
- Postcards
- Disneyana
- Movie memorabilia
- Retro and kitsch
- Science fiction
- Sporting memorabilia

"Everything I buy is vintage and smells funny. Maybe that's why I don't have a boyfriend."

Lucy Liu

Boot sale fever

chapter 4
Boot sale fever

And we're off! Look out, here I come! So is it off to a collectors' centre, auction or shop? No, stop! Start small and build up. Car boot sales are most definitely the place to begin before venturing further afield (pardon the pun). Take a look in your local newspaper and find out when the next boot sale takes place. These are always a good place to start because the chances are you might find something that is a real steal, rather than paying over-the-top prices.

You are still new to this game and given that everyone makes mistakes, you need to make sure yours are small ones and not too expensive by buying from boot sales first. Then, when you have increased your knowledge you can go up a notch and spend a few more pennies in the comfort of knowing you understand the market and recognise what you are looking at.

The day before

The first thing you need to do is be prepared. The day before your little adventure check the local newspapers to make sure that the boot sale is definitely on. The weather is a big defining factor and if it has been raining heavily the chances are the boot sale will be called off. The organisers usually give a telephone number so you can ring just to double check.

The early bird catches the worm

Set your alarm clock. Most boot sales start as early as 6am and
in order to get a bargain you need to be there with the best of
them. Although, some lucky people have found treasure later
into the day.

At one car boot sale my partner, Paul, discovered a rare Robert
Harrop plaque at 11am for which he paid £3 and sold for £620;
and my friend, Su, bought an original Beatles alarm clock and
vanity set from a dealer late morning, who believed it to be
reproduction. Su had them authenticated by a London auction
house as the genuine articles.

Be prepared

It's amazing how much time you can waste deciding what to
wear, so try to get your gear together the night before. You
don't want to be tripping over things in the dark or waking up
other members of the household who aren't so keen on joining
you on this little adventure. Wear layers of clothing so that if
it starts off freezing you have your winter clothes on but if the
sun comes out you can strip down to your summer garments.

Happy feet

Footwear is important too, you can cover miles trudging around fields so wear comfy shoes or your sore feet will make you want to give up and go home.

Handbag or rucksack?

Another thing to consider is the bag that you will carry. You want somewhere to put any goodies that you discover but you don't want to be too laden down and you need to keep your hands as free as possible. I suggest either a backpack or, like my friend Su, a trolley. Don't tell her I said that, though, because I always moan about her choice of luggage as it squeaks its way round the boot sale!

A pocketful of change

It sounds silly but actually it's very important. Make sure you have plenty of coins in your pocket or purse before going to a boot sale – it could mean the difference between bagging that elusive bargain and losing out completely. I have seen buyers approach a seller at the crack of dawn with a £20 note. There is no way a seller is going to be able to change that when they have only just stalled out. So if they can't change the note they will probably not sell you the item, which paves the way for other potential buyers who have been sensible enough to bring coins. They will be smiling all the way home whilst you will never forgive yourself for not pocketing a load of small change.

Treasure hunt

You're suitably attired, with a rucksack strapped to your back and a pocket jangling with change. The doors have opened and hoards of people are paying their entrance fees then flying around the stalls hunting out an early-morning bargain. Where do you start? Usually I head for where the people have already set up, I just can't bring myself to nose in the back of people's car boots before they have had a chance to get their items out – to me it's just plain rude. I prefer to have a leisurely hunt through boxes under tables and scour the treasures on show. There is always something that a dealer or another buyer has missed in their hurried effort to run around each stall.

Beat the dealer

As I explained earlier, many bargains have been found late into the morning so don't panic that the dealers have been there first. Chances are they were looking for things that you probably wouldn't have considered. Many excellent finds have turned up towards the end of a boot sale. One lady, for some reason, was drawn to a tea-stained Japanese watercolour and bought it for £7. Thankfully the dealers had ignored the painting all morning and when the lady took it to her local auction house it sold for £1,800. A rare picture by a well-known artist Yoshio Markino, it turned out to be only half of his painting – imagine the price if she had found the other half.

It just goes to show that there are ways of beating the dealer, just be prepared to look for unusual items and take a chance – it may well pay off.

Trash or cash?

One man's trash is another man's treasure.

A saying so true, when it comes to boot sales. Always spend time looking at the items on offer, the seller could have been a collector himself who has decided to downsize the collection or alternatively could have inherited a load of items that he cannot house. There is always something for everyone, so do not discard the boxes on the floor, have a rummage, and make sure you look at the items not so well displayed. Some of my best buys have been found in boxes of junk.

Wheeling and dealing

Even dealers' stalls can hide some hidden treasure as not everyone can know everything, so don't ignore the masses of dealers who set up each week. One of my best dealer stall bargains was a 1950s Marx Brothers boxed 101 Dalmatians Disneykins set. Haggling him down from £18 to £15 I walked off smiling as this rare find was worth in excess of £100. The dealer knew it was old and had some value but hadn't checked or researched it properly to find its real worth.

Cracks, chips, restoration or damage

It is common sense really but it only takes a few extra minutes to examine your potential purchases properly. This is paramount when purchasing from boot sales as, once you pay for an item and take it away, there is almost no chance of getting your money back. You probably will never see the seller again but even if you did, what proof do you have that you purchased the piece from them?

Top quality or second?

I have been caught out in the past when I have bought a piece of ceramic only to get home and find out it was a factory second. With Moorcroft there is a silver line put through the maker's mark, Portmeirion scratches a cross through theirs and with Royal Doulton the middle of the backstamp has been drilled. Run your fingers across the base to make sure there are no ridges where the factory could have made this piece a second and examine it properly to satisfy yourself that it is of first quality.

A fair price

Don't pay over the odds. Everyone thinks they are an expert as there is such an abundance of television programmes, books and internet sites where information is at the fingertips. Just because a piece has a well known maker's mark does not mean that it is worth the price the seller wants. Recently I was at a boot sale and a couple had a pair of boxed Palitoy Worzel Gummidge and Aunt Sally dolls. Yes, it's unusual to see them boxed but the lady wanted £50 for the pair. This would be well over the odds as they are only worth around £25 tops. She had a letter from a so-called expert who stated they were worth the £50 asking price but after some phone calls I realised this woman was no more expert than the seller. Sadly, the lady really believed their worth and would probably never get the price she wanted.

The chances are, if the price for something is high on one stall you will find exactly the same another time for half the price. Hold out; wait until you find the item you are looking for at a fair price. Don't get stung just because you have to have that item now!

Record-breaking bootsale booty

We all hear those stories of lucky people hunting out hidden treasure at a bootsale, such as the dealer who paid just £10 for a rare Charles Ashbee Claret Jug only later to sell it at a leading London auction house for £8,500. Another tale is of a gentleman who, after sorting through a box full of junk costume jewellery on the table of a bootsale stall, discovered a man's Jaeger Le Coultre watch. Handing over the £1 asking price he was pleased as punch because he was aware that this watch was worth in excess of £3,000.

However the best Bootsale Booty story is that of a couple from Tamworth in Staffordshire. They were attending their local bootsale when they spotted a crowded stall. People were snapping up pieces of attractive pottery quicker than the seller could get the items out. Cursing themselves for not arriving earlier, the seller then delved into the back of his van and pulled out more items which contained a colourful teapot. Catching the buyer's eye he handed over the £2 that the seller wanted. However, it was over eight months later when the buyer of the teapot noticed a similar one in an antiques magazine. Taking the teapot to a London Auctioneers, it was confirmed that this £2 buy was a rare 1878 Minton cat and mouse teapot. Placing it into sale this amazing bootsale purchase sold for a staggering £32,400, making it one of the best bootsale booty buys ever.

Childhood nostalgia

We all wish we owned the original Action Man and accessories, or kept our 1970s Star Wars figures in their boxes but there are other toys that you can find quite easily if you really hunt. Sindy dolls from the 1980s have a following, although the earlier ones from the 1960s and 1970s command more money. I have a friend who was doll mad and just a year ago on a very wet day together we discovered a stall covered in naked arms and legs belonging to about 10 different Sindys. We paid £1 for the lot. Amongst this collection of Sindys was a rare Patch doll (Sindy's sister). One week later at another boot sale we discovered Patch's original outfit for £1. So this doll had cost £2 in total. It was some time later that we were informed that the patch on the doll's outfit was a rarity as it was sewn onto the right knee. Most Patch dolls' outfits had the patch on the left knee so this outfit was more sought-after. The £2 spent was immediately turned into £110 rather than the £35 expected.

Keep your eyes peeled for anything associated with childhood memorabilia. There are many things to consider in this category, from children's television, film and book character collectables through to more traditional toys and board games. Rummage through the books, too, as you never know what might be lurking. Another friend discovered a 1970s collector's edition of The Hobbit for £3, which is easily worth £300-£350.

Just recently I purchased a job lot of vintage 1960s/1970s Action Men and accessories for £50. Now my knowledge of these boy's toys is limited but my instinct paid off as they were worth £120-£150.

Ceramics and glass

Everyone loves ceramics and glass and the better-known makers such as Midwinter, Beswick, Royal Doulton, Caithness and Whitefriars command a premium at boot sales, so you're better off looking out for less familiar names. I recommend Kathie Winkle's 1960s ceramic designs, or 1950s and 60s Murano art glass.

There are many factories that have not yet come up in the popularity stakes but which will certainly have their day. Troika Studio Pottery and Whitefriars glass was almost ignored ten years ago, now you have to part with £100s to own a single example. Try and look for things that are not yet moneyspinners but which have the potential to become sought-after in the future.

The vintage lady

A vintage lady at heart, I just love clothes and handbags from days gone by. My best buy was a Vivienne Westwood 1980s skirt for £1.50 which I found on a rail of modern high street store clothing. You can still pick up nice examples if you are prepared to trawl through the rails or search amongst the bags.

Vintage handbags are classed as the must-have accessories at the moment and occasionally you do come across one. Another thing worth looking at is shoes, all my boots are vintage and all have been bought at a boot sale for as little as £3-£5. Not only do they look good but you are wearing the real McCoy as opposed to cheap high street reproductions.

Haggle or be haggled

Haggling is one of my favourite pastimes and it's what people expect at boot sales. So once you have found a piece you want to purchase, give your haggling skills a go. It's a difficult thing to do first time round but with time it will become second nature.

Don't be greedy though – if the item is only £1.50 just pay the price. Haggling over 50p is both cheap and embarrassing. You already know you have a bargain and the seller doesn't want to give the stuff away. So, hand over your pennies and walk away, a contented seller and a happy buyer makes good bootsaling.

Winner or loser?

Whatever you come home with – you have bought things that you love. You are the winner and the loser is the person behind you that just missed out on the bargain. The other great thing about boot sale booty is that when you get home you can admire and research your items. There is nothing more satisfying than scouring the internet to find out information about your purchases and, who knows, you may well have a really good buy!

Booty hunting

Your first boot sale experience should kick start that must-have adrenaline rush. Hopefully you will discover a few good buys to satisfy your collecting appetite or you may even have spotted something that opens up a whole new mindset. Whatever happens you are now well on your way to contracting 'collectavitus' and 'boot sale mania' is just around the corner.

Our best boot sale buys

Here are some of the other top buys that my friends and I have had in the past few years.

- A 1930s Chad Valley Mabel Lucie Attwell designed Bambina doll for £35 and worth over £100.

- A sterling silver trophy cup bought for £10 and sold for £80.

- A Netsuke Japanese ivory carving bought for £65 and sold for £200.

- A Wade seal corkscrew bought for £15 and sold for £50.

- A pair of enamel art deco powder compacts bought for £10 and worth £85.

- A collection of vintage Action Men with accessories – £50 worth at least double.

- A ladies Escada pinstriped trouser suit bought for £15 and sold for £365.

- A vintage Topaz Yellow dial telephone bought for £5 and worth £30.

- A Harrods 2005 Christmas bear costing £18 and worth £25.

- A 1980s Space Fantasy Sindy doll for £4.50 and worth £25–£30.

> Collecting is a curious mania instantly understood by every other collector and almost incomprehensible to the uncontaminated.

Louis Auchincloss

Charity shop check-out

chapter 5
Charity shop check-out

U nless you are a really seasoned boot-saler like myself
and are able to visit between four or five sales a week
then you will definitely get withdrawal symptoms, this is
also true of the winter months when the boot sales have
come to a halt. So one of the other options for satisfying
those urges is your local charity shop which can uncover,
on occasions, some real gems.

Money tree

I am a firm believer in giving to charity, so please do not
misinterpret the tips that follow as advice on how to 'rip-off'
charity shops. It is just from a collector's point of view, a great
way to rummage, learn and find the odd bit for your collection
without paying over the odds for things. In the end the charity
shop benefits because if you find bargains then you will keep
going back to the shop to spend even more. This ensures that
the money goes round full circle and everyone is happy.

Charity shop or collectable centre

Antiques and collectables are big business and, with that in
mind, some charity shops now employ specialist valuers who
sort the wheat from the chaff before the goods even hit the
shop. If the good stuff does make it on to the shop floor it can
be very overpriced, but things often get missed, leaving the way
clear for people who really do know their onions.

The best things come from smaller shops

Rather than heading straight for the larger well-known charity shops try out the smaller ones first. These are usually much cheaper as they tend not to use valuers but instead rely on their own instinct, thus ensuring you can find a nice little bargain.

> **FACT**
> In 1949, the first ever charity shop to open its doors in the UK was Oxfam on Broad Street in Oxford.

Basket buys

These can usually be found outside the charity shops as they are deemed to hold items of very little value, such as children's toys. Well, we all know how huge the collectables market is for nostalgic items and toys are top of the list. I have often discovered an old Sindy or Barbie doll for as little as 50p, or a selection of vintage Lego just waiting patiently in the basket ready to be bought. So make sure you rummage through to see if there is anything to add to your collection.

Visit regularly

With masses of goods being donated every day, charity shops constantly restock, so there is always something new on the shelves. Make sure you make regular visits or you may well miss out on those bargains.

On a recent foray into a charity shop I discovered a boxed 2001 Border Fine Arts resin tableau of Soft Landings by Anne Wall. The price tag was £10 so the shop owner had recognised the name and given it a fair price but in reality this figure is actually worth £30-£35 on the secondary market. Don't be put off if something is priced more than a couple of pounds because it could still easily be a bargain buy.

Are markings a must or not?

The reason people are able to easily identify 20th Century products, especially ceramics, is because they are clearly marked on the base with factory name and sometimes the date they were produced. True experts are also able to identify much earlier pieces because of the quality of the workmanship, the designs and on occasions the obscure factory marks. This is where charity shop valuers tend to get things a little wrong.

A good friend of mine is a regular to his local charity outlets, having many amazing buys. One noteable find was an early fine English porcelain Caughley coffee jug which he instantly recognised by the serif and fake Worcester mark, snapping it up for the £2.50 asking price and later selling it on for £800 at a leading London saleroom. Another buy was a Vienna Cabinet Plate which carried the beehive mark on the back. Paying just £4, my friend was well aware that this stunning plate was worth nearer £1,000. It just goes to show that the more extensive your knowledge, the greater your likelihood of finding something really special that others have missed.

FACT

The Caughley Factory was famous for its blue transfer printed wares but they also produced some hand painted enamel decorated pieces which are much rarer.

Change around

If you are worried about being seen in the same charity shop too many times and thus being recognised as a possible dealer by the staff – don't panic! Most charity outlets rely on volunteers to man their shops so there is quite a turnover of staff.

Window shopping

I have often seen something I want in the window of a charity shop when it is closed. Panic stricken, I set the alarm early for the next morning and dash to the shop praying that I get there in time to buy the item I have seen. The trick is simply to slip a note under the door telling the shop you want the item and most of them will put it to one side until you get there to buy it.

Being an obsessed handbag collector I couldn't believe it when I spotted a 1960s poodle handbag in a charity shop window when it was closed. I dashed back the next day and was lucky enough to get my bag for £8.

It costs nothing to ask

Some charity shops sort their items on the premises so if there is something that you are looking for such as dolls or handbags, just ask if they have any more. There may well be some treasures lurking in the back which haven't made their way on to the shop floor yet!

One charity shop I visited used to let me loose out the back to see if there was anything I was interested in. It's amazing just how much stuff there is still to go on the shelves.

It's who you know

The other trick is to get friendly with the staff and let them know that you collect something in particular. They will get to know you personally and then put to one side anything they think may be of interest to you.

Privileged postcodes

Once you have become more confident about checking out the charity shops then check out the ones in the more affluent areas of big cities. These tend to stock better quality items, especially when it comes to clothes, shoes and handbags and you can find designer names at high street retail prices. A friend of mine purchased a Hermes scarf for £1 from a charity shop in a rich area and another great buy was a Gucci bag for £45 which would easily cost over £100 elsewhere.

Chapter summary

By now you should be slowly gaining confidence on your collecting area. You know what you want, have discovered a few pieces and have not parted with too much cash – but the craving is still not satisfied. Don't worry, we have only just touched the tip of the iceberg and used the boot sales and charity shops as a training ground. Now it is time to really compete with the hardcore. So get ready, you are about to step up a notch and really come head-to-head with other dedicated passionate collectors who want the same things as you and are willing to do battle to own them.

God help us if we ever take the theater out of the auction business. It would be an awfully boring world.

A. Alfred Taubman

Auction etiquette

chapter 6
Auction etiquette

The auction arena is most definitely the place to squash that collectables craving. Not only will you find absolutely anything and everything connected with the collectables market but you will also have fantastic fun. The excitement and atmosphere in the room, combined with the adrenalin rush that you get when bidding is second to none. You will also gain a great deal of knowledge by handling the items up for sale and meet many people who can advise and point you in the right direction. Here are a few tips to ease you into the exciting world of auction sales.

Which auction is best?

The first thing you need to do is find out where your nearest auction house is. You can search the internet for details, check in local newspapers or simply ask around. There are usually a couple within your area and other more seasoned auction goers will be able to advise you on which one may suit you best.

Quick tip

Register with the website **www.antiquestradegazette.com**. This is one of the most popular sites used by both auction houses and buyers. It has information on lots offered for sale, prices achieved, auctions that are happening worldwide, and regular auction news.

General sales

It's probably best to visit a general sale first. Consisting of everything from toys to glass and ceramics to furniture, there is such a range of items on offer that it is likely there will be something to take your fancy. General sales are also great places to get chatting to other auction goers who can advise, help you bid and teach you auction etiquette. General sales are a good place to build your confidence before venturing out to the larger prestigious salerooms around the country.

Estimates and reserves

Once you have found an auction you want to attend, and either looked at the catalogue online or requested a hard copy (normally costs anything from £3 to £30) from the auction house itself, then you can really understand how pricing works. There is an auction estimate beside each lot and this is what the auctioneer or valuer believes the item will sell for.

A pre-sale estimate of £80-£120 is a guide price, so to be in with a chance bid over the lower estimate. The lower price is usually the seller's reserve and unless that is met the item will go unsold, although most auction houses do have a 10 per cent auctioneer's discretion, meaning the item can be sold for £72.

These are simply guide prices, though, and it has been known on many occasions for an item to substantially exceed its estimate. Such as, the Jeffries concertina squeezebox in one of our sales at Stacey's. Estimated at a mere £30-£50 this musical instrument actually fetched £4,255. These items are known in the auction world as 'sleepers' and are often found in salerooms adding to the excitement.

Never bid without viewing

Once you have found a few things in the catalogue that you are interested in, you will need to view them before attempting to bid. Every auction house, whether it be one of the more prestigious London salerooms or a provincial sale will have viewing days before the actual sale. This is simply when all the lots (items) are on view for potential bidders to handle and examine. This is also a great way to learn, as you are handling items that you may well never see again and it gives you a great insight into what a piece looks and feels like.

Buy as seen

Auction houses stress an item is bought as seen, so if you do not view before you bid and it turns out there is damage or something doesn't look quite right you are stuck with it. So, where possible, make sure you take the time to view properly.

One gentleman made the mistake of bidding on a Japanese Netsuke piece without actually viewing it. After settling his bill and collecting the piece he found that it had been broken and badly glued back together, so he had paid for a worthless item.

Condition counts

Alternatively if the auction is miles away from where you live but they have something you desperately want to own you can request a condition report. This is where the auctioneer will supply you either by email or on the phone with an in depth report on any damage, hairline cracks, size or anything that you want to know about the piece. They can also date it for you and give you advice on whether the price estimated is fair or not.

Useful auction terms

- Gavel – the hammer used by an auctioneer.
- Porter – a person who holds up the items for sale so the buyers can see them.
- Paddle – your personal bidding card.
- Marriage – when two pieces of furniture are put together and don't match.
- Harlequin – a set that isn't quite a set; e.g. four chairs with one that doesn't look quite the same as the other three.
- Mint or near mint – when an auctioneer believes an item to have little or no damage.
- Foxing – mainly used when describing damage marks to a metal piece such as silver.
- Fresh goods – means that the item has come from a private person rather than through the trade.
- Provenance – the history of a piece.
- Pre-Sale Estimate – a guide price of what an auctioneer believes an item is worth.
- Sleeper – an item that has a low pre-sale estimate and is worth much more.
- Bidding off the Wall – an auctioneer can legally take a bid from any method necessary (such as off the wall) until he has met the reserve price.
- Off the Book – an auctioneer bidding on behalf of a potential buyer who has left a bid against a lot with the auctioneer.
- Price Realised – the price that something was sold for.

Cracked, grazed or chipped

As with everything in life, there are exceptions to the rule. Usually I would advise not to buy anything that's damaged but this doesn't apply if something is very rare. The prime example being the Lenci figures that I have already mentioned. Although I was aware of the slight damage to each I knew that this would not affect the price, as the demand for these 1930s art deco Italian figurines is high. So even though the nude lady on the hippo (Nudino Su Ippopotamo) had a slight chip under her nose, it did not stop her from realising £4,600, and the goose that had been knocked off and badly glued back on to the Nude in the Pond still sold for £1,900. My vendor (seller) was still in shock a week later when collectively the three pieces that she had placed into auction sold for in excess of £10,000. I was thrilled, as not only did I have a good sale but also I was in a position to handle items that I may never come across again. Most items, however, especially modern collectables are severely affected if damaged, so only bid on something chipped or cracked if you know it to be hard to find or alternatively if you just have to own it no matter what!

Ready to register

Before you can place any sort of bid you will need to register with the saleroom, which simply means supplying your personal details. Once this is done, you will then be given your own paddle number (bidding card). This number is unique to you and is what you will use to bid on any items of interest.

Set your limit

When buying, never forget that auction rooms are a business and have to earn their income from the buyers' and sellers' premiums. These are added to the final price and usually mean an additional 15-20 per cent on top of the hammer, although some of the bigger auctioneers charge as much as 25 per cent. Plus there is VAT to pay on the premium, so before you even attempt to bid make sure you know exactly what you are going to pay. For example if you have seen something and you are willing to go to £100 for, then you have take into account a 15 per cent charge which means you are paying £115, plus the VAT which makes that one piece then cost £117.62. It is important to calculate all the charges and then set your price.

People so often get carried away with the auction atmosphere and adrenalin rush that they get caught up in bidding thus paying way too much for things. This happened when I was bidding for a set of late Freda Doughty Royal Worcester figures. Luckily I bailed out at the right time but it could have been a different story.

Commission bids

If you are a little nervous about bidding in the room for the first time there are alternatives. The first is to leave a commission bid. This is where you leave the maximum bid you are willing to go to on the auctioneer's book. The auctioneer then bids on your behalf. This is the best way to start if you have never attended an auction before, as you won't go over your limit and often you win the item cheaper, as the bidding may stop with you at £65 rather than the £100 maximum that you left.

Telephone bidding

It is possible to take part in an auction without actually being in the room. You ask the auction house to set up a telephone line with you for a particular lot, then about five lots before yours is due, a representative from the auctioneers will phone you and tell you what the item is selling for. You tell the representative when you want to come into the bidding and they will bid for you. This system is used only when someone can't attend the auction but is desperate to own an item. It can be a very successful bidding technique as you are still bidding in order to secure the item for yourself but are not being persuaded or put off by the people bidding against you in the room.

One lucky seller rescued a 1920s Louis Vuitton travelling trunk from a skip. It was in terrible condition and the years of dirt and grime had covered most of the famous monogram LV pattern. However when placed into auction the telephone bidding was frenzied and this chance skip find made a staggering £1,800 hammer price.

Bidding in the room

There is no doubt about, actually bidding in the room is by far the most exciting experience you will ever have. The adrenalin rush is amazing and you really do get involved with the atmosphere of a buzzy sale room. When a lot comes up that you are interested in you simply attract the auctioneer's attention by waving your paddle But BEWARE this can be when you get so carried away you end up going home with armfuls of stuff that you paid over the odds for or on the positive side, some real bargains.

Fitting the gap

When planning on buying furniture at auction make sure the piece that you purchase will fit in your home. Measure up the space you want to fill, then at the viewing day measure the furniture that you are interested in. I know of someone who bought a gorgeous settee and armchairs for the conservatory. Unfortunately when the furniture was delivered it was far too big to get into the house, let alone through to the conservatory. So the buyer had to place the items back into the auction sale before she had even used them.

Transportation

When buying from auction, another thing to take into consideration is transportation. Now, this generally only applies when you purchase bigger items, however just make sure you have the means to take the item away, otherwise you could be charged by the auction house for delivery costs. This will again bump up the amount that you pay if you are lucky enough to secure the item at the sale.

You won!

If you are successful in winning a few bids, then you take your paddle number to the sale office where your account will be run off. Simply pay, usually cash, cheque or card and receive your collection slip to go and pick up the items you were successful with. Smiling all the way home with your arms full of goodies, you are a fully fledged auction addict ready to take on the best when it comes to auction sales.

My best buys

Obviously working for a saleroom has its ups and downs. I get to see nearly 1,000 goodies every month waiting to be snapped up. The downside is spending my wages before I have received them. Even I get disappointed when I am outbid but sometimes I win and that's when my partner groans as I turn up with even more collectables to fill the home with. Here are some of items I have purchased at auction for bargain prices.

- A Gabrielle Paddington Bear and Gabrielle Aunt Lucy for £80 (Aunt Lucy alone is worth the £80).
- A Tretchikoff painting of Miss Wong – £30 (£60 in any top London shop).
- A collection of 5 Royal Worcester Freda Doughty figures – £60 (bargain)
- Most of the designer furniture from the Big Brother house (sad, I know!).
- A vintage crocodile handbag - £85 (satisfies my handbag fetish).
- A Merrythought mohair Christmas 2005 teddy bear – £30 (worth £70).
- A collection of Sindy doll outfits for £80 (I love clothes, even dolls clothes).
- A Troika marmalade pot for £55 (usually around £70 to £85).

"People always say congratulations. When you're a successful bidder it means you're willing to spend more money than anyone else. I'm not sure if that's congratulations or condolences."

Eli Broad

Internet auction shopping

chapter 7
Internet auction shopping

Once you have the basic know-how for bidding at auction why not try your hand at one of the internet auction sites. You have to be careful, because in internet auctions you rely solely on the seller's knowledge and honesty for information and an accurate condition report on the item you're interested in. But the added attraction of bidding on these sites is that you can do it from the comfort of your own home, at any hour, 365 days a year, then just sit back and wait for the postman to arrive – it's like Christmas every day!

Be aware

Internet auctions sales have many advantages for buyers but things can go wrong. For instance, the seller might not be honest and you may never receive the item you have paid for; or if your bargain buy does arrive it has been damaged in the post due to poor packaging and to top things off the seller doesn't offer a refund policy. Also with this industry you don't want to be paying large amounts of cash for fakes.

You are depending on technology and the honesty of other people behind their computer screens for a smooth easy transaction.

It's all good

Don't let the odd disaster story regarding Internet buying put you off, though, because 99 per cent of people are honest and you will get what you paid for or if you lucky, slightly more because you managed to bag yourself a bargain. We've all heard stories of people getting the most amazing bargains from internet auctions, so let's hope you get to become part of that circle as well.

A few years back my partner purchased a Highland Fling Royal Doulton Snowman figure for his collection on an internet auction site. The seller then emailed to say that the red colouring from the figure's kilt was missing so would understand if he wanted to bail out of the sale. When the figure arrived, I took it and had it authenticated at Royal Doulton, who confirmed its authenticity and, as I had suspected, the fact that it was a one-off oddity.

When my partner decided to sell off his collection of snowman figures, the Highland Fling purchased for £85 sold for a staggering £800, purely because it was an unusual piece.

How to start

Obviously the first thing you need is a computer, otherwise you may as well skip this chapter altogether, but once you are technically equipped then the world is your oyster. Check out the auction sites and find the one that is best for you. There are a few to try but go for the ones that have the best reputations, such as eBay.

Feel around the site

Before you even attempt to bid, make sure you know your way around the site first. Read its policies, check out some items that may be of interest and find out exactly how the site works.

Feeling confident

Once you are fully confident with the site and feel that you are ready to dabble the first thing you need to do is register. Ensure you have set yourself up with an email address. These are free from most internet service providers, so just find one that suits you best and create your email account.

Then, just like a regular auction house, you need to register with the internet auction site. This mainly consists of finding a user name that is unique to you and creating a password so that no-one else can bid in your name. Then there is the usual filling out of personal details – simply follow the instructions.

> **FACT**
> The advantage to buying from internet auctions is that, unlike normal auction houses, there is no buyer's premium, so you don't pay any extra hidden costs.

Credit or debit

You will need to place a credit or debit card on file when registering with the majority of internet auction sites. This is a perfectly safe environment to use your card, so don't worry. It ensures that you are who you say you are and then you can pay for things through the PayPal service (see *Hooray – I won!* page 94).

Ready, steady, go!

Once you are fully registered and ready to bid it's worth taking time to get a feel for the site first. Internet auctions are fantastic for looking for additions to your collection. They have so much on offer and this is usually where you will find that must-have item. There are many sub-categories when it comes to the collectables section and here you will find absolutely everything from pottery, glass, dolls, bears and books to breweriana, kitchenalia, die-cast toys and postcards. Almost every collectable category that has ever been in existence can be found on these sites.

Price check

A really sound tip is to get an idea of the sort of prices that the item you are after sells for. For example: if you are looking for a rare Corgi, 1965 James Bond Aston Martin car then you sign into the site using your user name and password, search Corgi James Bond and then hit the 'Completed Items' button at the side. This will then show you all the Corgi James Bond cars that have sold over a period of time and what sort of price they achieved. So you know roughly what you need to pay. It's a great forum for keeping an eye on market trends because an item is only worth what a person is prepared to pay.

Check out the seller

Before you place your first bid, read the description of the item properly. If you are unsure of something in the description then contact the seller to confirm any points that you need clarified. Another important factor is to make sure that the seller is reputable. This is done by clicking on to the number next to their user name which will give you the seller's feedback rating. This is the best way to suss out if the seller is genuine or not. Their feedback score will tell you everything you need to know about the seller, if they have a high feedback rating with many positive remarks then you can more or less guarantee that they are genuine, honest people.

Postage and packing

Before you get carried away bidding on all sorts of goodies it's a good idea to check the seller's postage costs. If you are buying something heavy then the postage on that item can be extremely high, so just decide what price you are prepared to go to, including the cost of the item being shipped to you. If you are buying from overseas you may get hit with customs charges, sadly there's nothing you can do about this – it's payable when the postman delivers your item.

Insurance

Most sellers offer to send your parcel through the post by recorded or special delivery. Make sure, where you can, that you pay that bit extra for insurance because at least then you know you will get the money back if the item is lost or damaged.

Refunds and returns

Check before bidding that the seller offers a full refund policy so if you are unhappy with the item when it arrives you are able to send it back to the seller for a full refund.

Bidding mania

Quite confident that you know how much to spend, have taken the postage costs into account and ensured that the seller is legitimate – now is the time to place that bid. This is really easy, just click into the item, read the description then hit the 'Place bid' button, this will then ask you how much you want to bid (internet auctions use proxy bidding which means the bidding goes up in increments so make sure you enter your maximum amount). Once you are happy with the amount you wish to place, you press the confirm button and are now part of the big world of internet bidding.

I always look at international sites but have been caught a couple of times with customs charges. The first was for a stunning Llewelyn 1950s Lucite handbag which I bought for £85, the customs bill was £50 so in fact the bag ended up costing £135. Another time, I bought a designer watch for a fraction of its price here in the UK but even with the customs charge it was still cheaper than buying in the local high street. Make sure that even if you do get customs charges you are still saving money from purchasing in the UK.

Outbid

If you have placed a bid of say £10 and a message comes back that you are outbid then that means that someone else has entered a higher amount than you. Either enter another amount or simply walk away and find the same item somewhere else on the site. Just make sure you don't get carried away and end up paying way too much for something as, like boot sales, you will find another one at your price level.

In it to win it!

If you know that you are going to be sitting at your computer when the auction draws to an end then I suggest waiting until the death to bid. The auction ticks away in seconds so if you can contain the excitement make your maximum bid in the closing minute. This will give you more of a chance of actually winning.

Want it now!

Some auction sites allow you to post a 'Want it Now' message. This is great because if you're after something in particular, like a Jessie Tait Zambesi coffee pot to complete the 1950s coffee service you have been collecting, then you can just let people know you are looking for it. Simple to use you, just register what you are looking for and then post the message in the hope that people will get in contact with your much desired item.

Fat fingers

There are many ways of securing yourself a bargain and as a reputed internet auction queen I will let you into a few secrets. The first is a genius site **www.fatfingers.com** which is dedicated to finding those items that sellers have misspelt in their listings. So for example if you are looking for Sindy doll items, the seller may have spelt 'Sindy' as 'Cindy'. This site will then find all the wrongly spelt items for you which ensures your chances of winning these items is higher because very few other people have found them.

Italian or English

Look out for items that have been mis-described by sellers. Sometimes sellers make mistakes by either putting the wrong title for a piece or listing it in an irrelevant category. This paves the way for the clever buyers to swoop in and buy something at a bargain bucket price.

The classic case was when a seller listed a cream boat on an internet auction as being made by the Italian company Capo-di-Monte. One lucky buyer realised the seller had made a mistake with the manufacturer as it was not Capo-di-Monte but actually a very rare moulded relief piece of Royal Worcester. Successfully winning the item for around £250, the buyer took the cream boat to Bonhams saleroom in London for authentification. Dating to 1752-1753 this particular design by Royal Worcester was only the second example recorded so went on to sell for a staggering £36,800 (inclusive of buyer's premium). The initial seller had made a major mistake by not researching and finding out exactly what it was he had to sell.

Snipe for me

If you haven't the stamina to stay up all night waiting to bid or even if you are not around for the auction finish then you can register with an auction sniper site who will bid on your behalf; www.auctionsniper.com is one of the most popular and as with the auction you enter the highest amount you want to bid to and the sniper will do it for you.

Late night shopping

Here's a great way of really grabbing those bargains. Many international sellers have some amazing collectables on offer and of course the USA and Australia have items ending in the very early hours of our morning because of the time difference. If you have the stamina to stay up late then this is the best time to bid. Log on to the international sites to see what is on offer. Of course there will be some competition from the international sellers themselves, but most of the European buyers will be safely fast asleep. The other added bonus is that people are still a little nervous about purchasing from overseas so competition is not as high, which should result in you securing an item for a much cheaper price than you may have had to pay by purchasing from a UK internet site.

Worldwide sites

Check out other country's internet sites because you will get some great additions for your collection. Recently, I went on to the German internet auction site because I was looking for Schuco toys. Yes, everything is written in German but you can see from the picture that the item is of interest. Then you simply copy the German description and paste it into a translator. Then you can read all about the item and bid if you want it.

I bought a Schuco Tricky Monkey by translating the description then asking the seller questions in German, again using a translator. Normally this monkey would have cost at least £100 if I was to buy in the UK but I won him for £42. So using a little initiative I saved myself over £50.

The odd and even rule

Most people tend to bid in round even numbers, £10, £20, £30 and so on, but one of the best ways to stand more of a chance of winning is to bid in slightly different increments. So rather than £10 place a bid for £10.02. That 2p could mean the difference between you winning your collectable or losing out.

Hooray – I won!

The internet auction sites usually run for a number of days, but if at the end of the auction you are successful and have won the item that your heart desired then the seller and the auction site will contact you via your email address to let you know. Then you simply complete the check-out by telling the seller how you will be paying. My tip is joining up with **www.paypal.co.uk** which is an internet site where you register and can pay using a debit or credit card. This site also covers you should the item get lost or damaged in the post so you can claim your money back from the seller. It is just an added protection so you definitely won't get ripped off. If you don't want to use your cards, then in the UK you can pay by personal cheque or postal order, but overseas payments are slightly more complicated and can end up costing you a lot in bank charges so PayPal is the recommended form of payment if buying from overseas.

Feedback

Make sure once you have received your item and are happy with it that you leave positive feedback for the seller. This is really important as the seller and you, the buyer, rely on this feedback rating to build up your reputation on the site. Make sure you pay for the item promptly and then you too will receive a glowing feedback report and build up your rating quicker.

Chapter summary

Your internet shopping experiences should be a stress free and exciting adventure, so now you know a few tricks of the trade, you should end up with a problem-free transaction.

- Buy yourself a computer which has internet access.
- Sign up for an email address.
- Check out the internet sites and get a feel for them.
- Register so that you can bid on the site.
- Check out market prices so that you don't pay over the odds.
- Ensure the seller is genuine with a glowing feedback rating.
- Use one of the sneaky tips for securing a bargain.
- Bid your maximum amount, preferably near the end of an auction.
- When you have won pay the seller promptly.
- Ensure you leave positive feedback if happy with the item you receive.

> I collect antiques. Why? Because they're beautiful.

Broderick Crawford

Collectors' & antique fairs

chapter 8
Collectors' & antique fairs

Even though you can source items on the internet, attend live auctions and check out the cheaper option of boot sales and charity shops there is nothing more enjoyable than spending the day browsing round a traditional antiques and collectors' fair. The introduction of internet auctions has made life hard for the dealers that depend on stalling out and selling their stock, so go and have a look to see what they have on offer – you will be surprised at how much there is.

Where to start

As always consult your local newspaper, there are collectors' fairs all over the country and the smaller local ones are the perfect place to hunt out your collectable items.

Trade for that treasure

Many fairs open their doors an hour or two earlier for the trade then allow the public in later. You have to pay slightly more for this privilege but it is worth the extra few pennies as you might get your hands on something that could well be sold by the time the public are allowed in.

Keep those eyes peeled

You never know what you will find on a stall as some of them sell a cocktail of items from ceramics and teddy bears to advertising memorabilia and glass. Have a good scan and make sure you haven't missed a little treasure that is hiding at the back of the shelves.

One of my favourite buys was a 1930s diet tin. It sounds bizarre, I know, but the tin decoration epitomised the era and inside were loads of lovely little cards with diet plans and images of ladies exercising. I paid just £15 – a real bargain for something so unusual.

Instinctive buying

As with any kind of collectable buying, always go on your own instinct. We can't possibly remember the price of every item but if you feel in your bones that you should be buying something – then do!

I was at a very small local fair a few months back and noticed a Harrods 1987 Christmas teddy bear. This range of bears started in 1986 and are extremely sought after but, especially, with the 1986 version there are fakes on the market. Although my instinct told me to buy him, I was a little unsure whether this particular one was genuine or fake so decided not to. My mistake, because the lady only wanted £8 and when I arrived home to check on an internet auction I realised it was genuine and was selling for £45 – I should have gone with my first instinct.

Specialist advice

Stall holders are more than happy to enthuse about their passion so don't be afraid to probe them with questions. Many like to share their knowledge so are happy to give you any advice if you are unsure on something.

Get to grips

Wandering around a fair you feel like a child in a sweet shop. There is so much on offer so take time to take it all in and get an idea of what you are interested in. Don't rush to buy, because chances are you will find something else you desperately want on the next stall, and the next, and the next!

Providing provenance

Whenever you purchase anything, especially if it has some age, make sure it has sound provenance. This basically means find out as much as you can about the item's history. Ask if the seller knows anything about where it came from and if there is any paperwork to back it up.

For example I purchased a Venini glass decanter which belonged to Elton John. I knew this was true because the decanter had the original Sotheby's Elton John sticker on the base and when I checked on the internet I found the original auction lot number and sale catalogue. All proving, that this particular piece was not just any Venini decanter but actually owned at some point by the singer.

Summer months

My favourite fairs are the ones in the summer that open up for outside stalls — this is where the bargains can be found. All the outside sellers have usually turned up in the morning on the off-chance that the weather will be good and there will be plenty of buyers. It is at these stalls where you will find a whole wealth of goodies from books to dolls, bears to ceramics etc. So rummage round these first before entering the hall to look at the more expensive, quality items.

At my local Brentwood fair I found a stall that was selling every character collectable I could think of at discounted prices. It was fantastic because I added to my collection of Royal Doulton Bunnykins figures and bought a few extra bits that normally would have cost quite a bit more.

Waiting list

Always ask if you are after something in particular but can't see it on the stall. You never know, the seller may have failed to unpack this piece or simply forgotten to bring the item to the fair. Then you can get their details and arrange to buy it from them at a later date.

Reference section

You will usually find a big book stall at the fair and these generally have wonderful reference books on every subject imaginable. Make sure you save some time to browse through the books to see if there is anything that will help you on your quest to finding more items for your collection.

Deal or no deal

Never be afraid to ask the price if you can't see a ticket. If you can't afford it then just walk away but dealers usually offer up to a 10 per cent discount so find out what their best price is first. You never know, you may end up with a really good deal.

Dealers need to make a living too

When it comes to haggling at fairs make sure you don't go too far. This isn't a boot sale where people are just trying to get rid of their belongings; this is a serious business where the dealers rely on their sales as an income. Just remember that they need to make a living so do not haggle by offering stupid money.

Put aside for me please

Sometimes you might see something you desperately need to own but do not have enough funds with you. Most dealers will take a deposit and hold onto the item for you, then you can either pay once you have visited the bank or send the money to them.

Spend wisely

Prices are normally nearer the market value at fairs so only buy it if it is a good price or it is something that you have been looking out for. Unless of course you have absolutely fallen in love with it and don't care how much you spend. I have a passion for anything girlie and at one of the big London fairs was instantly attracted to a powder compact. Normally I won't part with more than £50 but I just had to own this particular one and so I was more than happy to hand over the £80 to secure my little treasure.

Cheque, cash or card

Make sure you take enough money with you when attending collectors' fairs. Most dealers accept a cheque with a guarantee card and some now accept credit cards, but you don't want to lose out on something because you haven't enough cash funds with you.

Fair or centre

The same tips above apply to collectable centres which are spread all over the country. These shops can house real treasure and are usually open on Saturdays and Sundays, as our passionate hobby is a sociable weekend affair. So check out your local centres to see if there is anything that can help you expand your collection.

Receive a receipt

Make sure you ask for a receipt when you pay. This is just a precaution in case you find something wrong with the item when you get home that you hadn't noticed or the seller didn't point out. This rarely happens but just be on the careful side.

My friend purchased a 1972 Wade Tom and Jerry figure from a stall at roughtly the going price, because the seller had confirmed they were both in mint condition with no damage. When he looked more carefully my friend realised one was badly chipped. Luckily he returned the item to the seller and was given a full refund but had to show the receipt as proof of purchase.

Specialist events

Specialist events and fairs are held across the country so if you have a particular area of interest, find out where and when these take place. You can choose between vintage fashion, art deco, toys, postcards, glass and dolls, to mention just a few.

Look and learn

Even if you do not have a particular specialist interest then it is still really advisable to attend some of these fairs. It is amazing how much you can learn by just looking at all the other things on offer. For example you may not find that record fairs appeal, but if on a rainy afternoon you fancy getting out, go and take a look. You might have no interest in vinyl but you may well see an LP that triggers off happy memories and then this in turn will lead you into another collecting phase as it opens up your mind to the areas connected with records, such as album covers, music memorabilia, or just plain old nostalgia.

Chapter summary

Collectors' fairs are one of the more traditional routes for hunting out treasures, so you usually have to pay the going market rate rather than securing yourself a bargain. In return, however, you will have spent an enjoyable day browsing the stands and seeing the range of items on offer. If you're lucky you may spot a piece that you have been after for a while or simply did not know existed.

"Thank God we are living in a country where the sky is the limit, the stores are open late and you can shop in bed thanks to television.

Joan Rivers

High street hiding places

chapter 9
High street hiding places

Now this really is a treat, because even when out food shopping at your local supermarket you will be able to indulge your hobby. It is unbelievable what can be found as you trail around the shops on a Saturday morning. I have had some of my best buys from the most unexpected places. So pay attention, because now you can shop 24/7 for those treasures – although you may have to hide the carrier bags in the wardrobe or under the bed when you get home.

Why the high street?

Quite simple really, literally everyone is cashing in on the limited edition phenomenon. Collecting covers all areas and some of these can be found easily in your local department stores or smaller gift shops. So when you are next out shopping for a new bottle of perfume or a glass vase for the home, take note of all the other wonderful items on display.

Sale mania

Just the best times of the year – when the shops have a sale. This is where you really will bag a bargain! Head for the big department stores which offer the best sale discount and you can buy armfuls of designer bags, ceramics, glassware, clothing, homewares, cosmetic and jewellery at the cheapest price.

The sweet smell of success

Perfume bottle collecting, including modern scent bottles, is classed as one of the most popular collectables categories. Instead of just reaching for your usual brand of perfume next time you are in a department store, look to see what else is on the shelves. Many cosmetic houses now release limited edition scents and compete to have the most design-innovative shaped bottles. Collecting perfume bottles, especially popular ones is a top category and the more unusual the bottle, the higher the chance of it becoming sought after. The recent influx of celebrity-endorsed perfumes has added to the attraction of perfume bottle collecting.

Crazy compacts

Ladies powder compacts also rank high on the collecting table. Many collectors are after vintage ones that date to the 1920s and 1930s through to the 1980s but others tend to concentrate on modern examples. Explore the cosmetic counters in the department stores because one of the biggest names in modern compact collecting is Estee Lauder, who release special limited editions at Christmas, although the really unusual ones can only be found in London's department store, Harrods.

Christian Dior is also well known for releasing wonderful limited edition compacts throughout the year. These have become very popular, so get in quick, find out when they are being released and snap them up.

Bags of style

I love handbags, and some of my all-time favourites are the designs of Lulu Guinness. Taking vintage influences and combining them with more contemporary design, Lulu has a range to suit all tastes. You can choose between one of the more adventurous limited edition bags that are made exclusively for the collector's market or from one of her seasonal collections which are released around three times a year. Whatever your preference you will not only be buying a piece of fashion history but something that has collectable appeal all over the globe.

Quick tip

When going on holiday check out the duty-free shops because there are stores that stock all sorts of collectable items such as Lulu Guinness handbags, plus you can get limited edition cosmetic items from foreign duty-free shops and other exclusives on the aeroplanes themselves.

Designer items for high street prices

If something has a good name it will always hold its value and collectability. Some shops now offer top designer brands at more affordable prices. So make sure you have a good rummage, because you never know what you might find tucked away. I purchased a gorgeous Emilio Pucci handbag for a third of the original £300 retail price from one of these designer discount stores and my friend snapped up a Lulu Guinness handbag for a similar bargain price.

For free

At Christmas many perfumeries offer free gifts if you buy their scents. These gifts alone can become highly regarded by collectors so as the festive season approaches, have a look to see which freebies have collectable appeal.

A few years ago I purchased Vivienne Westwood's Boudoir perfume which came with a free canvas bag. A good designer name, both the bag and the bottle soon became popular with collectors.

Every Christmas Georgio Armani bring out an annual teddy bear which is given away free with their perfumes. These gorgeous teddies are sought after in their own right.

Getting on the "A" list

The problem with all these limited edition specials is that they sell out really quickly. The secret is to make friends with the girls behind the cosmetic counters and get them to give you the nod when the next one is going to be released. Really nice staff will even ring a few days before the item is due in store to ask if you would like one put by.

Sold out!

Obviously with anything that is high in demand, chances are you will not be lucky enough to get everything that you want. This is where the internet auctions come in really handy as if you are unable to secure one from a store I can guarantee you will find it on the internet, although usually at a premium. If you want it badly enough you will be willing to pay the price.

Designer names

Top collectable designer names to look out for ...

- Anya Hindmarch
- Balenciaga
- Chanel
- Christian Dior
- Gucci
- Emilio Pucci
- Estee Lauder
- Hermes
- Issey Miyake
- Jean Paul Gaultier
- Julien MacDonald
- Karl Lagerfeld
- Lulu Guinness
- Manolo Blahnik
- Matthew Williamson
- Philip Treacy
- Radley
- Versace
- Vivienne Westwood
- Yves Saint Laurent

Charity case

Items that you buy to raise funds for charity have developed their own collecting field so make sure you look next to the cash till to see if there is anything on offer that falls into the collectables bracket and you will also be helping to raise money for charity.

In 2005 the women's clothing store Wallis released a charm bracelet to help raise funds for Cancer Research UK. Each charm was designed by a celebrity and the bracelet sold out really quickly making them hard to come by now. In 2007 the same chain store released a charm necklace, once again for charity. Costing £25 it had designs by Catherine Tate, Christian Louboutin and Kate Moss to name a few. So keep a watchful eye out for any charity items that could become collectable in future years.

In 2006 the designer Anya Hindmarch released a limited edition canvas bag in conjunction with the environmental charity We are What we Do. The idea was to produce a re-useable bag to stop people from buying plastic carrier bags as they seriously harm the environment. The demand was phenomenal and when released in the UK people were queuing for hours outside the participating supermarket to obtain one at the £5 retail price. (Including me – I was there at the crack of dawn.) These bags began to exchange hands for hundreds of pounds on the internet for quite a long period after the release.

Celebrity fashion

Many high street stores now stock lines designed by well-known celebrities. The first collection by Stella McCartney had people queuing round the block to snap up her garments, and then came Madonna's collection and a line by supermodel Kate Moss. Some of these outfits (especially if the tags and carrier bags are stored away) will no doubt be classed as the collectables of the future by fashion enthusiasts.

Homewares

Most of us at take for granted the everyday items that surround us. It's worth looking more closely at the kitchenware and homewares on our shelves because collectable gems can be found. Among my favourites is Alessi which produces some of the most unusual designs in homewares, especially for the kitchen.

> **FACT**
> Alessi designer Michael Graves, launched his Whistling Bird kettle in 1985. This kettle sold into over 1.3 million homes worldwide. Even now Graves is asked to sign his kettle, much like an author does his books.

VIP

Habitat has a VIP category which includes all sorts of homeware products designed by famous people, many of which are names associated with the collecting field. Keep a watchful eye on the store as the desirable items, such as the Manolo Blahnik shoehorn, sell out quickly and which command a premium on internet auction sites.

Glassware to ceramics

You can discover all kinds of glassware and ceramics in some of the designer discount stores if you look hard enough. Although you have to rummage, this is a great way of finding a little treasure. I bought an Italian vase by the glassworks Handle With Care who produces designs by the iconic designer Ettore Sottsass for just £17. Another great buy was a large Murano glass dish for just £25, this glass is becoming a hot bed for collectors at the moment so is certainly worth popping one or two bits in your collection.

Free for all

When walking around your local supermarket it is unbelievable what collectable goodies you can find. Remember the Lurpak butter toast rack, egg cups and butter dish – well these all now slot into people's collections. Then there was the Wallace and Gromit nose colour changing mug which came free with teabags – people were clearing shelves trying to get their hands on one of these collectable mugs. So make sure you keep your eyes peeled when doing the week's shopping as you never know what you may find.

Coupon collecting

If the item doesn't come free on the shelves, then you can collect tokens or coupons which entitle you to claim a freebie. The Andrex puppy dog was one collectable toy which you received if you sent off the correct amount of tokens and we all remember the Robertson Golly badges that people collected, well some of the rare ones can be worth over £100 now. So buy the product, save the tokens and claim your collectable.

Weird and wacky

Another thing to check out on the supermarket shelves are weird and unusual items. As mentioned before many manufacturers have jumped on the limited edition bandwagon and this goes for food items as well. Not so long ago the company 'Canderel' teamed up with four fashion designers and asked them to create labels for the front of the sweetener packets. Matthew Williamson, Patrick Cox, Giles and Julien MacDonald each came up with amazing designs for these limited edition packets of 'Canderel' sweeteners. Although originally they were only available through Harrods, they did go nationwide afterwards. Each pack proved popular with collectors, especially those who collect fashion items or are intrigued by packaging – so it became extremely difficult to obtain all four designs. My tip is when next in the supermarket make sure when looking for your usual brand that there isn't a limited edition designed package hidden amongst the regular packaged items.

Chapter summary

Retail therapy is always rewarding but especially so when it indulges your passion for collecting. I hope I've encouraged you to seek out treasures in places that you might otherwise have ignored. Bear in mind that these tips can also be put to good use when you're travelling abroad because many manufacturers offer different products in other countries. So now you can carry on collecting while food shopping or even when browsing the hypermarkets abroad.

Recently I've been collecting Star Wars figures again. When I was a kid I couldn't afford them. Now I can so I've been buying them and keeping them in their box for a later date when they'll be worth a lot of money.

Mackenzie Crook

Collectable kids' stuff

DO NOT TOUCH

chapter 10
Collectable kids' stuff

As children, many of us owned a collection of some sort – for me it was stamps, coins and marbles. Today children like to exchange football cards and stickers, all hoping to secure the rarest and hardest to find to complete their collection. Part of human nature, this instinct for collecting material things starts at an early age and, for many people, carries on throughout their lives. So what could our children start collecting?.

Furry friends

Bears have always been a favourite with adults and children, so this is one of the categories I suggest you consider for the kids. But with hundreds of different bear manufacturers where do you start?

Good makers such as Steiff, Merrythought, Deans and even the artist bears I mentioned in an earlier chapter are always worth a look, but remember these bears can be very expensive so are not classed as toys but collectables that should be loved and cared for.

Once a year

Each year manufacturers bring out special items that tie in with key dates of the year. Look out for special collectables produced only at Christmas, Valentine's, Easter, or Halloween.

Beanie or bust

Beanie Babies were huge some years back with everyone frantic to get their hands on as many as possible. Sadly, many black bin liners are now hidden in people's attics stacked full of these furry bean filled teddies and animals. A short-lived collecting frenzy meant that some avid collectors spent thousands of pounds buying every beanie they could, only to find now that you can't give them away. It's a lesson for us all... although we don't buy for investment, we don't want to throw money away. So stick to an established area for your children which will bring fun and enjoyment and hopefully be a lasting collecting area that they can reap the benefits from in the future.

Character collectables

We all remember our favourite children's storybook or a film that brings back memories of our youth and this is a massive area of interest for collectors. You can purchase all sorts of related memorabilia from vintage to modern contemporary designs. Beatrix Potter is probably one of the top contenders, but there are many others from Tom and Jerry through to Paddington Bear.

Dolls

Once again, there are hundreds of different dolls around, from the fashion examples to the baby dolls. If you're starting a collection for your little girl, try and avoid the mass-produced fashion dolls and go instead for those that are produced in smaller edition sizes or available only from certain retail outlets. Each year Mattel releases a range of Barbie Collectable dolls. Although a little more expensive than the average Barbie, these really are special but can be found only in the big stores, such as Hamleys in London.

Disneyana

There can't be many people who haven't watched a Disney animation film and this is an excellent area for children's collections. Disneyana crosses many different collecting subject headings, from ceramic figurines and cuddly toys to pin badges and film cells. You'll find all sorts of associated products and companies such as Disney Classics produce ranges of porcelain figurines which are dedicated to the characters from Disney films. Some of these figures are limited editions so are worth buying now as they should become more desirable as the children grow up.

Petrol head

Boys just love fast cars and there is even a collectable that covers this passion. Created by Terry Ross, Speed Freaks! are the ideal shelf filler for any little boy's bedroom. Made of resin these wacky caricature model cars are highly collected, and once you have bought the cars you can also purchase the looney figures that go with them.

Imaginative items

Aside from the well-known commercial licensed products, many collectable manufacturers also offer make believe characters. The Royal Doulton Bunnykins figures I collected as a child are still produced today and are the ideal collectable for children. The three-dimensional figures were first introduced in 1972, although the original illustrations date back to 1934 when Barbara Vernon's delightful humorous rabbits were reproduced on to nurseryware.

Hummel figures are also perfect for children. Like Barbara Vernon, Sister Maria Innocentia Hummel created drawings of children which were then modelled into figurines by the German manufacturer W. Goebel. These are widely available from gift shops around the world and would make a lovely gift for a child and the perfect introduction to collecting.

Wonderful Wade Whimsies

You can't talk about collectables without mentioning the British Wade factory. Many of you will remember the pocket-money ranges of Wade Whimsies and even today Wade is constantly producing new ranges of these characters. Varying from Felix the Cat to Betty Boop and the Gingerbread Family to Gingie Bear there is something for boys and girls, with a whole lot more to choose from.

> **FACT**
> CS Collectables have all the latest releases from Wade including special commissions and limited editions, so are one of the best retail outlets for this pottery.

Sticking with stamps

Buckingham Covers (see also *Stamp Collections* on page 45) who produce autographed stamp sheets and first-day covers are definitely one of my top tips for children's collectables but don't be tempted to buy just any first-day cover. The most common mistake with modern cover collecting is to buy them from Royal Mail. They may be cheap and cheerful but they are not a sound investment and many collectors have found out that, after years of collecting, their collection is worth far less than they believed it would be.

- Go for the signed covers with signatures relevant to the theme of the cover.

- Make sure the signature is genuine. Some companies sell pre-printed signatures, whilst Buckingham Covers' signatures are all authentic and original.

- Store them safely in folders so that they will not get damaged or dirty.

- Buy them because you love them – but choose carefully and your collection just might increase in value.

FACT

In 1979 Benham Covers released a Winnie-the-Pooh cover signed by Christopher Milne, the son of Winnie's creator A.A. Milne, and the original Christopher Robin. A tag that dogged his life, after Milne had signed the covers he made it perfectly clear that it gave him no pleasure to be associated with this famous bear. This cover recently sold for £175, a far cry from its original price of £3.

Memorabilia

Another recognised collecting area for children is memorabilia. This incorporates everything from television and film to sport and music. So if your little boy is football mad take a look at the masses of memorabilia associated with the sport but go for things that are a celebration of a sporting date in history or related to an iconic player.

Quick tip

When attending any sporting or music event, make sure you keep hold of your entrance ticket as these can become more sought after than the event programmes.

The same goes for television and film. Doctor Who has made a popular comeback to our screens recently and as a result there are plenty of boxed toys and figures dedicated to this sci-fi programme – anything that has longevity or covers more than one collecting category is always a good place to start.

In the films category, it's the big blockbuster movies that spark off many collections, especially films that are popular with both children and adults. Find out what is on offer that has collectability. A recent film that has recaptured the hearts of collectors is Transformers. The Generation 1 figures dating back to 1984 were released in conjunction with the original television programme and are already selling as collectables at auction houses. The new ones may, in time, be just as collectable.

Budding bookworms

Great children's authors such as J.K. Rowling, Roald Dahl and Enid Blyton already command huge premiums if you are lucky enough to own a first edition of their books. And this makes an excellent collecting area for children. Not only will they experience the same level of fun which is gained from collecting other items but they will also enjoy and learn lots by reading the books. Make sure that they look after any special volumes, however, as the slightest damage to books can drastically devalue them – and this includes writing the child's name on the inside pages.

Useful book collecting terms

- Title Page – At the front of the book giving details of the author, publisher and date of publication.
- Recto – The right hand page of an open book.
- Verso – The left hand page of an open book.
- Proof copy – A sample copy of a book that the publishers and author can check before being printed.
- Plates – Full-page illustrations.

First editions

A good friend of mine is an avid First Edition Book Collector. He spends hours looking for the rare examples and a fortune to acquire them. Time and money eventually paid off when he wandered into a charity shop. There on the book shelves was a first edition of Philip Pullman's *Northern Lights* (otherwise known as the *Golden Compass*). Published in 1995, only 500 were originally released at a retail price of £12.99 each. Handing over the £1 asking price he couldn't believe his luck as this particular book can command in excess of £1,000, as long as it is one of the original 500 which have the word 'POINT' on the jacket spine, and the address 7-9 Pratt Street on the rear flap.

Modern first edition book auction prices achieved in 2007...

- *Northern Lights* by Philip Pullman – sold for £1,900.
- *James and the Giant Peach* by Roald Dahl – sold for £600.
- *Charlie and the Chocolate Factory* by Roald Dahl – sold for £1,800.
- *James Bond Casino Royale* by Ian Fleming – sold for £20,000.
- *James Bond Dr No* by Ian Fleming – sold for £2,200.
- *The Island of Adventure* by Enid Blyton – sold for £140.
- *Harry Potter and the Philosopher's Stone* by J K Rowling – sold for £9,000 early in the year. However, a world record was achieved towards the end of that year when a rare fine copy of the same book sold for £19,700 at Christie's.

Child's play

Encouraging children to start collecting at an early age can set them in good stead for the future, and there are all kinds of educational advantages. They will learn how to appreciate things, understand the value of money and build an interest in something other than the television or the computer. Learning through their own collecting experiences will also help with learning life skills such as communication, organisation and record keeping.

Chapter summary

I have only touched the tip of the iceberg for children's collectables as there are so many other different areas out there to consider. The trick, as with any collecting, is to research an area first. Look at the suggestions I have made then think of what you collected in your youth. There is also price to think about. You want your child to be able to afford to purchase their collectable goodies themselves, so ensure that their pocket money covers the price of their chosen collecting area. Then of course accessibility; it is important that the children can easily get hold of the items they are interested in. There is no point in starting them on something that is hard to find, because otherwise they will become frustrated and, in time, uninterested with collecting. I believe that if you follow my tips and ideas you will find that there is something for everyone, which covers all price ranges and will be relatively easy to find.

"Mass-produced products are being created today that, once they are no longer in production, will significantly go up in value because they represent noteworthy design in their time."

Lisa S Roberts

Future
collectables

chapter 11
Future collectables

Okay, say it after me: "Only collect because you love it!" Well yes, I still stand by this maxim, but sometimes it is worth considering what might become valuable and sought after in future years.

My mum is always shocked at the things she took for granted over the years that have now become the collectables that we all have to own. Mum absolutely hates the Tretchikoff prints that I have on my walls and the Cornish Troika marmalade pot that has pride of place on my mantelpiece and she simply cannot understand the yearning I have for vintage 1960s clothing by Mary Quant or Biba. Why? Because she lived through these things and remembers them as cheap household items and the clothes she used to go out in.

It's a bit of a dodgy area, because nothing is guaranteed but if you use your trained eye to find a so called 'future collectable' it may pay off twice over. Not only will you enjoy owning it now but it could also increase in value in the future. So what do we keep a look out for? The answer is simple, classic designs and anything that epitomises the era we live in, even if it is only available for a short period. But don't go hoarding absolutely everything, be choosy and consider the suggestions below, because you need to use your instinct for this one as not everything will become a future collectable.

Potty about pottery

Many things are already classed as collectable but this doesn't necessarily mean that they have reached their peak yet. One of my other favourite pottery designers is Roger Cockram. Based in North Devon, his innovative pots are inspired by the colour, movement and texture of water. Although he is highly collected already I still feel, that his collectability has not reached it's peak and that in years to come Roger's work will be exchanging hands for considerable sums of money. My tip is to look for quality potteries that are producing today but will obtain the high level of recognition that they deserve in the future.

A touch of glass

The same theory goes for glass collecting. Look for British glass manufacturers who have a distinctive style. The designs from John Ditchfield of Glasform, although getting better known, are still not at their peak. His amazing iridescent, almost Tiffany-like designs are quality craftsmanship at its best and I believe his work will become even more sought after in future years.

A touch of bling

I just love anything 'bling' and there are many fantastic costume jewellery makers that are sure to become part of the elite circle in years to come. Check out the designs by Erickson Beamon and Lola Rose as these two, in my opinion, will surely make their way up into the collectors' market at some point. Always buy good quality pieces though, as these will stand the test of time.

Handbagmania

I just can't resist handbags and although I spend hundreds on vintage examples and invest even more cash in the more modern designs, there are many that you can buy now that have future collectable potential. So when next out shopping at a department store look at the designs by Matthew Williamson and Radley, who are already recognised names amongst collectors but still have the potential to become even more in demand in the future, especially designs that have long been discontinued.

Frivolous fashion

We all wish we owned an Ozzie Clarke dress, Mary Quant mini or a pair of original Vivienne Westwood pirate boots but these highly collectable fashion labels were not always as desirable as they are today. Look at high street brands and see if there is anything that sticks out as a possible future fashion must-have.

Once again, quality always has longevity so designer names will always be welcome but some of the high street store labels may also become desirable if the item of clothing has a distinctive look.

Quick tip

Try to buy some of the celebrity-designed clothing, wear it, look after it, save the bag, tags and receipt, then when you are bored stash them away for a few years.

Packaging

When it comes to everyday mundane items, look past the actual item itself and pay attention to the packaging. In 2007, I was asked to appear on BBC Breakfast to discuss the fact that the classic Campbell's soup label was being axed and replaced by a more modern looking design. This original label reached worldwide acclaim after being immortalised in Andy Warhol's art in the 1960s and can be found on all kinds of consumer merchandise. The fact that the label is now non-existent makes it achieve an even higher collectable status. So when considering packaging consider whether it is a design which epitomises an era or whether it has been a classic familiar to everyone. These factors form part of our social history and are often the key to an item acquiring collectable status.

Telephone telepathy

No one could have guessed that telephones would become as highly regarded as they are now. From the 1920s art deco period right through to 1980s there have been many classic designs that are now eagerly collected. So when you next pick up the phone to gossip to a friend take a little more notice – you could be talking into a future collectable.

On the move

The same principle goes for the mobile phone. The 1980s so-called 'brick phone' has already gained collectable status so who knows what the future holds for the technically enhanced models that we speak into today. Then of course, we cannot forget the MP3 players. I remember when the only portable music we had was a Walkman, now we can choose between a host of designs and colours in digital music appliances. My tip is whenever you upgrade; pack the old one away in its original box in the hope that one day you will be showing it off as an historic collectable.

Rock and pop

Whenever you attend a music concert ensure you purchase a programme and keep your entrance ticket. We are all aware of the prices that Beatles merchandise realises at auction, well the same may well happen for some of the merchandise for today's music icons.

Political prizes

Prime Minister, Margaret Thatcher, was one of the most influential political figures of the 1980s and thus was the subject for a great deal of memorabilia. Today, some of these Thatcher items can command a few hundred pounds especially if created by the ceramics factory Carlton Ware. Buying novelty political items may turn out to be a shrewd move, especially if they are of well-known politicians who have made an impact on our times.

Brands are best

Advertising is big business for collectors. Many major commercial companies use branded goods as a form as advertising, so don't be tempted to throw away that Coca Cola bottle opener or ditch the Cadbury's tin once you have devoured all the chocolates, they could become treasures instead of trash.

80s & 90s

1980s and 1990s objects worth collecting now...

1980s

- Mickey Mouse telephone.
- Atari and Sinclair computer consoles.
- Wade NatWest Bank pigs.
- Cabbage Patch Dolls, Care Bears and My Little Pony.
- Telephone cards.
- McDonalds toys.
- Swatch watches.
- 1980s Sindy Dolls.
- ET and Ghostbusters memorabilia.
- First mobile phones.

1990s

- Dauphine calculator.
- Commemorative ware of Princess Diana.
- Original Spice Girls memorabilia.
- Madonna 'Sex' book.
- Alessi Michael Graves Whistling Kettle.
- Oasis pop memorabilia.
- Pokeman toys.
- Tamagotchi games.
- Toy Story, Titanic and Pulp Fiction movie memorabilia.
- Nintendo Game Boy.

Iconic designers

If something has a good designer name to back it up then you are on to a winner especially when it comes to modern design. I personally favour Philippe Starck, a French contemporary designer who has produced hundreds of designs for furniture, lighting and homeware companies. However, there are many others to choose from. Starck's Louis Ghost Chair and Eros chair are design classics. They have also made appearances on television as they were used as part of the fixtures and fittings in the Big Brother house.

FACT

The Juicy Salif lemon squeezer designed by Philippe Starck for Alessi, was used to create a visual image of a space ship in the Men in Black film.

Chapter summary

The collector in us all cannot help but constantly be on the look out for things that may be deemed 'future collectables' – it comes as part of the package. Nothing is guaranteed though. Use your initiative and look more carefully at the everyday items around you, and decide on your own merits what you should store away and revisit in 10 years' time. You may well have a better idea than me about 'future collectable' possibilities but the fun element of this guessing game is that you won't know you've hit the jackpot until the demand begins at some point in the future.

> **Always care for your collection as one day your collection may financially take care of you.**

Mark Seaby

Caring for your collection

chapter 12
Caring for your collection

I hope that by now you can confidently class yourself as a collector and that during the course of reading this book you have tried your hand at internet auctions or perhaps just popped to the shops to see if there is anything that takes your eye. There are probably a few carrier bags stuffed under the bed waiting for you to find the right opportunity to tell your partner that you've started collecting! But there are also some serious matters to attend to, which include cleaning and taking proper care of your new treasures.

Ensure they are insured

Insuring your collection is a priority. Some of your collectables could be worth a few pennies and more importantly might be impossible to replace. You could just include your collection within your home contents insurance policy but eventually your collection could be worth more than your provider's home insurance cover. Should something unfortunate happen, general insurers are not always the best companies to deal with specialist items such as collectables.

It's a good idea to take a policy with one of the insurance companies which DOES specialise in this market and understand the collector's needs by offering all risks policies. This takes everything into consideration from breakages through to trading items with other collectors.

The essentials

When taking out insurance:

- Keep a list (spreadsheet) of all the items bought and price paid.
- Watch the market then create an up-to-date price list of how much it would cost to replace an item.
- Photograph every piece as proof of ownership.
- Store safely any receipts or paperwork in case the insurer asks to see it.
- Mark the bottom of each piece with a property marking kit.

Take care

Protecting your interests in other ways is also something you need to consider. Much damage can be caused if you have not stored the items properly. or if you leave them on display where they could become damaged by the elements. Take some time to read the following paragraphs to make sure you know exactly how to take care of your collectables.

Storage

Sometimes you may need to store your collectables. If this is the case encase them in bubble-wrap or acid free tissue paper. Plastic bags are a definite no-no as they can discolour items.

Light rays

Direct sunlight and even artificial light can be harmful, especially to textiles, toys and papers. So where possible keep your cherished items on display in a low natural light.

Steady temperature

Although we all do it, the loft, garage and shed are the worst places to keep your collectables because of the humidity changes. If something gets too hot, then too cool there is a danger of it cracking. If a collection gets damp this is also disastrous as mould or mildew can ruin the item. Try to find somewhere warm and dry to store those precious items.

Keeping it clean

It is not advisable to clean everything, although dusting ornaments is fine as long as you use a soft brush or damp cloth to gently clean the dust away from delicate areas. Most ceramics and glass can also been washed but only by hand in tepid water. Never place in the dishwasher.

Metal protector

Try not to clean metals, especially pewter, unless really necessary. Not only will you clean away the patina which adds extra kudos to an ageing piece but you could overclean and lose the essential hallmarks. If the hallmarks cannot be read clearly then the item is instantly devalued.

Quick tip

Cigarette ash is wonderful for cleaning silver. Dip your finger in an ashtray and gently rub the area which needs lifting. Using this process is a lot more effective then using abrasive metal cleaners.

Tip top toys

- Never overwind mechanical toys, they are easily broken.
- Store board games flat and keep all the playing pieces together so that they don't get lost.
- Only ever wipe over a doll with a damp cloth, or better still seek profession cleaning advice first. The same with teddy bears – never ever wash them. Don't store toys in a place where the sunlight can fade them or creepy crawlies can eat them.

Postcards and stamps

Keep all papers, including stamps and postcards in proper presentation folders, this stops any damage and keeps them clean.

Books

The same goes for books. Make sure they are not handled too much so that the spine doesn't get broken and the pages are kept pristine.

Handbags

Store them in the cloth dust bags that you receive when purchasing modern bags, this allows the bags to breath and keeps them in tip top condition. Also store away from direct sunlight as this can cause cracking to hard plastic and fading to fabrics.

Compact caring

Only use a soft cloth to clean compacts, never use abrasive metal cleaners as they can remove the protective film that is on the surface. Also do not be tempted to wash your compact in water, especially if it has a mirror, as the water will seep behind and once again damage the coating. An old toothbrush can be used to brush away excessive loose powder and a cotton bud dipped in methylated spirits is perfect for cleaning off sticky labels. Once clean only display behind glass if possible, as the vapours in the atmosphere can damage the surface of a powder compact.

Vintage clothing

Try to keep your vintage clothing items dust free but don't use a plastic bag to cover them. Throw in a sprig of lavender when storing as this acts as an insect repellent and keeps away nasty little creatures.

Chapter summary

Taking care of your collection is paramount. I have heard many stories about people's homes being broken into, only for the culprits to return at a later date to finish the job by stealing the homeowner's precious collectables. Then, of course, accidents happen and things get broken or soiled. We can't always prevent unfortunate things from happening but I hope you now know how to protect those items that are dear to you.

A final word...

So come on, fess up – how many of you have already contracted 'Collectavitus?' Yes, I thought as much, addiction is not a strong enough word is it? Don't worry though, it's a disease that gives you a warm fuzzy feeling inside and not one that leaves you feeling weak and unable to move – that is unless you are still reeling from the shock of spending a small fortune already.

I hope you have learnt at least something from this book and that I have encouraged you to jump on to the collectables band-wagon. Collecting is about having fun, gaining pleasure and buying things that you fall in love with. Then, of course, you will learn something new every day. In fact, at this very minute I am sitting surrounded by a collection of wonderful items that a seller wants to place into auction, a couple of which I have never been privileged enough to see in the flesh before– until now that is.

Whatever you have decided to collect, I guarantee that every bright new day will bring some sort of revelation, whether it be in the form of a collectable object or a piece of information that you were not aware of before. So put your new-found hobby into practice and get out there because you are now a fully fledged collector and there is no going back!

Tracy x

Acknowledgements

There are so many people that I need to thank, as all have contributed in one way or another to my life and in turn the writing of this book. (You know who you are.)

My special thanks go to the following:

To Eric Knowles for writing such a wonderful foreword and for his continual support which I very much treasure and to those from the industry who have shown equal amounts of encouragement and support, such as Mark Oliver, Stephen Moore and Mark Hill.

Huge thanks go to my friends and family who made it possible for me to turn my obsessive hobby into a career. To mum and dad for making me the collector that I am today, huge thanks to Lorne Spicer, for her continual encouragement and friendship, and to Helen, Nicky and Angie for being the best friends a girl could have. Thanks also goes to my boot sale companion Su, as without her car and chauffeur skills I would be unable to hunt out treasure every weekend. Not forgetting Julie Peasgood, who has literally turned my life into one big rollercoaster ride, and of course a massive thank you to Steve and Anne Brookes at The Greatest in the World Ltd., for making one of my dreams come true.

My biggest thanks, however, have to go to my beloved Paul, whose patience, encouragement and support have not gone unnoticed. Thank you for just being there, and allowing me to chase my dream. Without you I would be unable to live my passion. Love Always.

Useful contacts

MANUFACTURERS & RETAILERS:

Adam Binder Editions Ltd
Marston Hill Farm
Meysey Hampton
Cirencester
GL7 5LQ
Tel : 01285 711700
Email : adam@adambindereditions.com
www.adambindereditions.com

Buckingham Covers
Warrne House
Shearway Road
Folkestone
Kent
CT19 4BF
Tel: 01303 278137
www.buckinghamcovers.com

CS Collectables Direct Ltd
Victorian Business Centre
Ford Lane
Arundel
West Sussex
BN18 0EF
Tel: 01243 555371
www.cscollectables.co.uk

Dennis Chinaworks Limited
Shepton Beauchamp
Ilminster
Somerset
TA19 0JT
Tel: 01460 240622
Email : info@richarddennispublications.com
www.richarddennispublications.com/chinaworks

Dinsdale Petch,
Running Dog Art Foundry
4 The Square
Brayley Cross
East Buckland
Barnstaple
Devon
EX32 0TA
Tel : 01598 760558
Email: info@dinsdalepetch.co.uk
www.dinsdalepetch.co.uk

Direct Ceramics Limited
23 Boleyn Way
Hainault
Essex
IG6 2TW
Tel: 0208 5000345
www.direct-ceramics.co.uk

Echo of Deco
Unit 8-3-8 Harpers Mill
White Cross Industrial Estate
Lancaster
Lancashire
LA1 4XF
Tel: 0791 4733852
Email : info@echo-of-deco.co.uk
www.echo-of-deco.co.uk

(John Ditchfield) Glasform Ltd
Pointer House Farm
Fleetwood Road
Singleton
Poulton-le-Fylde
Lancashire
FY6 8NE
Tel: 01253 893020
Email : sales@glasform.com
www.glasform.co.uk

Isle of Wight Studio Glass Ltd
Old Park, St Lawrence.
Isle of Wight
PO38 1XR
Tel: +(0)1983 853526
www.isleofwightstudioglass.co.uk

Merrythought Ltd
Ironbridge
Telford
TF8 7NJ
Tel : 01952 433116
Email : contact@merrythought.co.uk
www.merrythought.co.uk

Okra Glass Studios
12 Queen Street
Wordsley
Stourbridge
West Midlands
DY8 5QW
Tel : 01384 271644
Email : okraglass@aol.com
www.okraglass.com

Robert Harrop Designs Ltd
Coalport House
Lamledge Lane
Shifnal
Shropshire
TF11 8SD
Tel:01952 462721
Fax: 01952 462972
Email: collectorsclub@robertharrop.com
www.robertharrop.com

MAGAZINES:

Antiques and Collectables
Gemini Publications Ltd
14 Queens Square
Bath
BA1 2HN
Tel: 01225 338773

Antiques and Collectables for
Pleasure & Profit
P O Box 655
St Ives
NSW 2075
Tel : +61 2 9983 9806
Email: info@accpp.com.au
www.acpp.com.au

Car Boot and Market Calendar
P O Box 277
Hereford
HR2 9AY
Tel: 01981 251633
www.carbootcalendar.com

Collect it! Magazine
Warner Group Publications
The Maltings
West Street, Bourne
Lincs
PE10 9PH
Tel: 01778 391000
www.collectit.info

Doll Magazine
Ancient Lights
19 River Road, Arundel
West Sussex
BN18 9EY
Tel: 01903 884988
Email: support@ashdown.co.uk
www.dollmagazine.com

Teddy Bear Scene
Warner Group Publications
The Maltings
West Street, Bourne
Lincs PE10 9PH
Tel: 01778 392011
Email: tbscomments@
warnersgroup.co.uk
www.teddybearscene.co.uk

AUCTIONEERS:

BBR Auctions
Elsecar Heritage Centre
Barnsley
South Yorkshire
S74 8HJ
Tel: 01226 745156
www.onlinebbr.com

Bonhams
101 New Bond Street
London W1S 1SR
Tel: 0207 629 6602
www.bonhams.co.uk

Chiswick Auctioneers
1 Colville Road
London W3 8BL
Tel: 0208 992 4442
www.chiswickauctions.co.uk

Christies
85 Old Brompton Road
London SW7 3LD
Tel: 0207 930 6074

Potteries Specialist Auctions
271 Waterloo Road
Cobridge
Stoke on Trent ST6 3HR
Tel: 01782 286622
www.potteriesauctions.com

Stacey's Auctioneers & Valuers
959 London Road
Leigh on Sea
Essex SS9 3LB
Tel: 01702 475614
www.staceyauction.com

Tennants
The Auction Centre
Leyburn
North Yorkshire
DL8 5SG
Tel: 01969 623780
www.tennants.co.uk

Vectis (Collectable Toy Specialist)
Fleck Way
Thornaby
Stockton on Tees
TS17 9JZ
Tel: 01642 750616
www.vectis.co.uk

INSURANCE:
Hiscox Insurance
Tel: 0845 345 1666
www.hiscox.com

Connoisseur Policies
www.connoisseurpolicies.com
Tel: 0870 2410 142

Michael James & Associates
335 Limpsfield Road
Sanderstead
Surrey
CR2 9BY
Tel: 0208 657 9948
Email: mja@steadmanhozier.com
www.mjacollections.co.uk

Index

P

Packaging, 20-21, 136
PayPal, 87, 94
Partner, effect on, 14
Perfume bottles, 110
Perfumeries' free gifts, 112
Political memorabilia, 137
Porcelain, 39
Postage & packing, 89
Pottery, 39, 134
Price, 56
Programmes, concert, 137
Provenance, 101

Q

Quality, 19-20, 55-56

R

Reasons against collecting, 14
Reasons for collecting, 13
Receipts, 104
Reference books, 28
Refunds, 89
Registering for auction, 77
Reserves, auction, 74
Resin sculptures, 43
Returns, 89

S

Sales, 109
Scent bottles, 110
Seller, internet auction, 88-89
Sniper, auction site, 92
Specialist events, 105

Specialists, 30, 101
Sports memorabilia, 46
Stamp collecting, 45, 125
Storage, 144
Sunlight, 144
Supermarkets, 116-117

T

Teddy bears, 43, 121
Telephone bids, 79
Telephones, 136
Television programmes, 28
Temperature, 145
Time limited, 38
Toys, 146
Transportation, 80
Trends, 18
Troika, 17

V

Viewing, auction, 75
Vintage clothing, 147
Vintage items, 59
VIP designed items, 115

W

Wade factory, 124
Workshops, 29

'The Greatest Tips in the World' books

Baby & Toddler Tips
by Vicky Burford
ISBN 978-1-905151-70-7

Barbeque Tips
by Raymond van Rijk
ISBN 978-1-905151-68-4

Cat Tips by Joe Inglis
ISBN 978-1-905151-66-0

Cookery Tips
by Peter Osborne
ISBN 978-1-905151-64-6

Cricketing Tips
by R. Rotherham & G. Clifford
ISBN 978-1-905151-18-9

Dog Tips by Joe Inglis
ISBN 978-1-905151-67-7

Etiquette & Dining Tips
by Prof. R. Rotherham
ISBN 978-1-905151-21-9

Freelance Writing Tips
by Linda Jones
ISBN 978-1-905151-17-2

Gardening Tips
by Steve Brookes
ISBN 978-1-905151-60-8

Genealogy Tips
by M. Vincent-Northam
ISBN 978-1-905151-72-1

Golfing Tips
by John Cook
ISBN 978-1-905151-63-9

Horse & Pony Tips
by Joanne Bednall
ISBN 978-1-905151-19-6

Household Tips
by Vicky Burford
ISBN 978-1-905151-61-5

Personal Success Tips
by Brian Larcher
ISBN 978-1-905151-71-4

Podcasting Tips
by Malcolm Boyden
ISBN 978-1-905151-75-2

Property Developing Tips
by F. Morgan & P. Morgan
ISBN 978-1-905151-69-1

Retirement Tips
by Tony Rossiter
ISBN 978-1-905151-28-8

Sex Tips
by Julie Peasgood
ISBN 978-1-905151-74-5

Slimming & Healthy Living Tips
by Wendy Green
ISBN 978-1-905151-31-8

Travel Tips
by Simon Worsfold
ISBN 978-1-905151-73-8

Pet Recipe books

The Greatest Feline Feasts in the World by Joe Inglis
ISBN 978-1-905151-50-9

The Greatest Doggie Dinners in the World by Joe Inglis
ISBN 978-1-905151-51-6

'The Greatest in the World' DVDs

The Greatest in the World – Gardening Tips
presented by Steve Brookes

The Greatest in the World – Yoga Tips
presented by David Gellineau and David Robson

The Greatest in the World – Cat & Kitten Tips
presented by Joe Inglis

The Greatest in the World – Dog & Puppy Tips
presented by Joe Inglis

For more information about currently available
and forthcoming book and DVD titles please visit:

www.thegreatestintheworld.com

or write to:

The Greatest in the World Ltd
PO Box 3182
Stratford-upon-Avon
Warwickshire CV37 7XW
United Kingdom

Tel / Fax: +44(0)1789 299616
Email: info@thegreatestintheworld.com

The author

Tracy Martin is an accomplished modern day collectables expert who specialises in today's current market but is also extremely knowledgeable about the collectables industry as a whole. She has appeared on live TV, radio, and conducted lectures and workshops; she has also been a special guest at open days for some of the biggest collectable companies around.

Tracy is also a Specialist Collectables Consultant for an auction house, and on a monthly basis, sources, markets, and sells items – both antiques and collectables. She is a regular contributor to many specialised collectable and antique magazines, including Collect it! and the Australian publication Antiques and Collectables for Pleasure and Profit.

The Greatest Collecting Tips in the World is Tracy's first book.